R Programming for Beginners

Master the Fundamentals of R, Even with
Zero Coding Experience

Peter Simon

3

Discover others in the Series

"R Programming for Bioinformatics: Analysis of Genomic and Biological Data"

"R Programming for Data Analysis:The Complete Beginner-to-Expert Guide to Unlocking Insights from Data"

"R Programming for Machine Learning:Building Predictive Models"

"R Programming for Statistical Analysis:Unlock the Power of Data-Driven Insights"

Disclaimer

R Programming for Beginners by **Peter Simon** is intended solely for **educational and informational purposes**. The content of this Book is designed to introduce readers to the fundamentals of R programming and to provide general guidance, examples, and best practices within the context of data analysis and related topics.

Introduction

Welcome to *R Programming for Beginners: Master the Fundamentals of R, Even with Zero Coding Experience*! This book is tailored for individuals who are either new to programming or looking to improve their analytical capabilities. R has become a vital tool for data analysis, statistical computing, and graphical representation, proving to be an essential resource for professionals in diverse fields such as data science, finance, and research.

In our increasingly data-centric society, the skills to analyze and visualize data are crucial. However, embarking on a programming journey can be daunting, particularly for those without any prior experience. This book is designed to simplify R programming, breaking down intricate concepts into easily digestible sections that will help you build confidence and develop your skills step by step.

We will start with the very basics—understanding what R is, how to install it, and how to navigate its distinctive environment. Following this introduction, you will delve into essential programming concepts, including data types, functions, and control structures, all explained in a straightforward and accessible way. Each chapter features practical examples and exercises, enabling you to apply your knowledge and reinforce your understanding. As we progress, we'll delve into data manipulation and visualization techniques using popular R packages. By the end of this book, you'll not only have a solid grasp of R programming but also the ability to analyze datasets, create compelling visualizations, and make data-driven decisions.

Remember, every expert was once a beginner, and the most important step is to take that first leap. You don't need to have any coding experience to succeed—just a willingness to learn and a curiosity about the world of data. So, grab your laptop, install R, and let's embark on this exciting journey together!

Welcome to the world of R programming—let's get started!

Chapter 1: Introduction to R and Its Importance

In the realm of data science and statistics, the capacity to analyze and interpret data is essential. As technology advances, the tools and programming languages utilized for data analysis must evolve to satisfy the needs of researchers, data analysts, and statisticians. Among these tools, R has distinguished itself as one of the most robust and adaptable programming languages for statistical computing and data analysis.

1.1 What is R?

R is an open-source programming language and software environment specifically designed for statistical computing and graphical representation. It was developed by Ross Ihaka and Robert Gentleman at the University of Auckland, New Zealand, during the early 1990s. The language is based on the S programming language, which was created for data analysis in the 1970s. Since its inception, R has experienced significant growth in popularity and has become a leading tool for data analysis worldwide.

R offers a comprehensive array of statistical and graphical methods, including linear and nonlinear modeling, time-series analysis, classification, clustering, and more. Its functionalities go beyond basic statistical operations, enabling users to produce impressive visualizations and efficiently handle large datasets.

1.2 Why is R Important?

1.2.1 Open-Source and Community Support

One of the most significant advantages of R is that it is open-source. This means that users can download and use the software for free, and developers from around the world can contribute to its ongoing improvement. The R community is robust and vibrant, making a wealth of packages, extensions, and libraries available for almost every statistical application imaginable. Biostatistics, bioinformatics, social science, finance, and marketing are just a few fields where R has found widespread use.

1.2.2 Comprehensive Statistical Capabilities

R's extensive statistical capabilities make it an invaluable tool for data analysis. It supports various statistical methods and paradigms and is continuously updated to incorporate the latest methodologies and discoveries. Whether it involves complex data modeling or advanced statistical tests, R provides the functions and capabilities needed to address various research questions and data challenges.

1.2.3 Data Visualization

Another area where R excels is data visualization. With packages like ggplot2, lattice, and plotly, users can create high-quality, publication-ready graphics easily. Data visualization is essential for making sense of complex data and effectively communicating findings to stakeholders. R's powerful visualization capabilities allow users to highlight trends, patterns, and anomalies in data, making it easier to draw meaningful conclusions.

1.2.4 Reproducibility and Collaboration

In research and data analysis, the reproducibility of results is critical. R promotes reproducible research practices through its integration with tools like R Markdown and Knitr, enabling users to create dynamic documents that combine code, output, and narrative text. This capability enhances collaboration, as researchers can share their findings in an easily understandable format while allowing others to reproduce and verify the results.

1.2.5 Integration with Other Technologies

R is not an isolated tool; it integrates seamlessly with other technologies and programming languages. For example, R can work alongside Python, SQL, and various big data platforms like Hadoop and Spark. This interconnectivity allows analysts to leverage multiple technologies within a single workflow, enhancing the power and flexibility of their analyses.

1.3 Applications of R

The importance of R extends across various domains. In academia, researchers utilize R for statistical analysis and data visualization in their studies, while in industry, companies rely on R to uncover insights from customer data, optimize operations, and drive business decisions. Sectors such as healthcare, finance, marketing, and public policy have all adopted R as a go-to tool for data analysis.

In healthcare, for instance, R is employed for epidemiological studies, clinical trial analysis, and genetic data analysis. In finance, analysts use R for risk analysis, portfolio optimization, and quantitative trading. In marketing, companies utilize R for customer segmentation and A/B testing to improve product offerings.

11

As we embark on our journey into the world of R, it is vital to recognize its importance in the field of data science. R's open-source nature, robust community, comprehensive statistical capabilities, and powerful data visualization tools make it an indispensable resource for any data analyst or researcher. Throughout this book, we will explore the various facets of R, equipping you with the knowledge and skills to harness its power for your data analysis needs.

The Power of R Programming for Technological Modernity

This chapter delves into the multifaceted impact of R programming on modern technological practices, emphasizing its role in analytical rigor, community collaboration, and the democratization of data science. As we explore the capabilities of R, we will also consider its implications for industries, education, and the future of programming as a whole.

The Evolution of R Programming

R programming, developed in the early 1990s by Ross Ihaka and Robert Gentleman at the University of Auckland, began as a project aimed at creating a free software environment for statistical computing. Its open-source nature has fueled an active community that continually enhances its capabilities through packages and libraries. This adaptability is particularly significant in an age where data is abundant and rapidly changing.

As we move into the era of big data, R has solidified its position as one of the premier languages for data analysis, visualization, and statistical modeling, making it a staple in both academia and industry. The seamless integration of R with databases, web technologies, and cloud computing has further established its relevance in modern technological environments.

R's Analytical Power

At the heart of R's appeal is its robust analytical power. The language excels in statistical analysis, providing a vast array of built-in functions for psychometrics, regression analysis, time series analysis, clustering, and more. R's ability to handle complex data structures, including data frames and matrices, makes it a versatile choice for data scientists and statisticians.

Moreover, the rich ecosystem of R packages—hundreds of which are available on CRAN (Comprehensive R Archive Network)—extends its functionality even further. Packages like `ggplot2` for data visualization,

`dplyr` for data manipulation, and `caret` for machine learning exemplify how R can meet diverse analytical demands. The ease of integrating these packages allows users to transition smoothly from data preparation to advanced modeling, showcasing the language's comprehensive approach to data science.

Visualization: Unleashing Insights

In the realm of modern technology, data visualization plays a crucial role in interpreting complex datasets. R shines in this area, offering sophisticated and customizable visualization capabilities. The `ggplot2` package, which adheres to the principles of the Grammar of Graphics, allows users to create aesthetically pleasing and highly interpretable graphics with minimal effort.

Effective visualization not only helps in exploring data but also aids in communicating results to non- technical stakeholders. By enabling the transformation of raw data into visual narratives, R facilitates informed decision-making across various sectors, from healthcare to finance. Interactive visualizations, made possible through packages like `shiny`, further amplify R's effectiveness, fostering real-time engagement and exploration of data.

The Role of Community and Collaboration

Another significant aspect of R programming is its vibrant community. The R community is characterized by collaboration, sharing of knowledge, and a commitment to open-source principles. Users around the globe contribute to and benefit from the continuous development of R packages and tools. This communal effort fosters innovation, as practitioners share new techniques, methodologies, and solutions to common challenges.

The annual useR! conference and myriad local user groups exemplify the collaborative spirit that underpins the R ecosystem. These gatherings inspire networking, learning, and the cross-pollination of ideas, empowering individuals and organizations alike to harness cutting-edge techniques and best practices. In an era where collaboration can lead to significant advancements, R programming exemplifies the power of community in technological growth.

Democratization of Data Science

As data analysis becomes increasingly critical in various industries, the accessibility of tools is paramount. R programming has played a pivotal role in democratizing data science, making it more accessible to individuals without extensive programming backgrounds. Its user-friendly syntax, coupled with the documentation and tutorials available within the community, allows newcomers to grasp essential data analysis concepts quickly.

Furthermore, with the advent of integrated development environments (IDEs) like RStudio, the learning curve associated with R has been significantly reduced. These environments provide user-friendly interfaces with powerful features that cater to both novices and experts. As a result, diverse professional fields—including marketing, education, and public policy—are incorporating data-driven decision-making practices, highlighting the transformative power of R in promoting analytical thinking.

Implications for the Future

As we look toward the future, the role of R programming in technological modernity will only expand. The continued integration of R with emerging technologies such as artificial intelligence, machine learning, and cloud computing will further amplify its relevance. Innovations in R, such as its enhanced capabilities for handling big data and its interoperability with other programming languages like Python, illustrate its readiness to adapt to future challenges.

Moreover, the emphasis on data ethics and responsible data use will influence how R is utilized in research and industry practices. As analytics drive critical decisions, a heightened awareness of bias and data transparency will shape the evolution of R programming and its applications.

By providing unparalleled analytical capabilities, fostering community collaboration, and democratizing access to data science, R has positioned itself as an indispensable tool for navigating the complexities of the modern data landscape.

Installing R and RStudio: Setting Up Your Environment

In the world of data analysis, statistical computing, and graphical representation, R stands as a potent tool. Its open-source nature and extensive package ecosystem make it a favorite among statisticians, data scientists, and researchers alike. To harness the full power of R, a user-friendly integrated development environment (IDE) is essential. Enter RStudio, an IDE tailored for R that streamlines coding, visualization, and productivity. In this chapter, we will guide you through the process of installing R and RStudio, ensuring you have a robust environment to traverse the fascinating landscape of data analysis.

Step 1: Installing R ### 1.1 Understanding R

R is a programming language and environment specifically designed for statistical computing and graphics. It offers various analytical functions, making it a preferred choice in academia and industry for data manipulation, statistical analysis, and producing high-quality plots.

1.2 Downloading R

To install R, follow these steps:

Visit the CRAN Website: Go to the Comprehensive R Archive Network (CRAN) at cran.r-project.org.

Choose a CRAN Mirror: You will be prompted to select a CRAN mirror, which is a server close to your geographic location. This ensures a faster download.

Select Your Operating System: R is available for various operating systems (Windows, macOS, and Linux). Click on the link that corresponds to your OS.

Download R:

Windows: Click on "Download R for Windows," then "base," and finally, click the installer for the latest version.

macOS: Click on "Download R for macOS," and download the latest version.

Linux: Follow the instructions tailored to your specific distribution (e.g., Ubuntu, Fedora). ### 1.3 Installing R

Once the installer is downloaded, proceed with the installation:

Windows:

Double-click the downloaded `.exe` file.

Follow the prompts in the setup wizard. You can accept the default settings unless you have specific preferences. This includes choosing the installation path and selecting additional components.

macOS:

Open the `.pkg` file and follow the installation instructions.

Linux:

Open a terminal and use your package manager. For example, on Ubuntu, you can run:

```bash
sudo apt update
sudo apt install r-base
```

Step 2: Installing RStudio ### 2.1 Understanding RStudio

RStudio serves as a professional IDE for R. It provides a user-friendly interface featuring a console, syntax highlighting editor, and tools for plotting, history tracking, and workspace management. RStudio significantly enhances your coding experience and is essential for managing complex projects.

2.2 Downloading RStudio

Visit the RStudio Website: Navigate to the RStudio official website at [rstudio.com](https://www.rstudio.com).

Go to the Download Page: Click on "Download RStudio" in the top menu. You will be redirected to the download page.

Choose Your Version: On the download page, you will

see different versions of RStudio—choose the "RStudio Desktop" version, which is free and suitable for most users.

Download for Your OS: Click on the appropriate link for your operating system to download the installer.

2.3 Installing RStudio

After downloading the installer, carry out the installation process:

Windows:

Double-click the downloaded `.exe` file.

Follow the setup wizard, accepting defaults unless you have particular requirements.

macOS:

Open the downloaded `.dmg` file and drag the RStudio icon into the Applications folder.

Linux:

For Ubuntu, you might run the following commands in your terminal (adjust paths and filenames accordingly):

```bash
sudo apt install gdebi-core
sudo gdebi rstudio-<version>.deb
```

Step 3: Verifying Your Installation

Now that you have installed R and RStudio, it's time to verify that everything is working as expected.

Open RStudio: Launch the RStudio application from your applications menu or desktop.

Check R Installation: In RStudio's console, simply type:

```R
R.version.string
```

If you see the version of R displayed, your installation was successful.

Test Basic Functionality: Type a simple command like:

```R
print("Hello, R!")
```

Press Enter. If it prints your message, everything is functioning correctly.

With R's extensive package capabilities and RStudio's cohesive interface, you are now equipped to embark on your journey into data science. In the subsequent chapters, we will delve into R's functionalities, including data manipulation, visualization, and statistical modeling.

Chapter 2: Understanding Basic R Syntax

This chapter will explore the basic syntax of R, helping you become comfortable with the language's structure and rules. By the end, you'll have a solid understanding of how to write and run simple R code, enabling you to delve deeper into data analysis and statistical modeling.

2.1 Introduction to R

R is a programming language designed specifically for statistical computing and data analysis. Its syntax is distinct but straightforward, which makes it both powerful and accessible for beginners. Understanding the syntactical rules of R is crucial for effective coding, as they determine how the language interprets your commands.

2.1.1 Comments

In R, comments are essential for making your code understandable to yourself and others. Comments are ignored by the R interpreter, allowing you to document your code freely. They are indicated by the `#` symbol:

```r
# This is a single-line comment x <- 5  # Assigns the value 5 to x
```

2.2 Basic Data Types

R supports several basic data types, which include:

Numeric: Represents real numbers (both integers and decimals).

Integer: Specifically denotes integer values (e.g., `1L` to indicate it's an integer).

Character: Used for text, enclosed in double or single quotes.

Logical: Represents TRUE or FALSE.

Here's how to define variables of different data types:

```r
num_var <- 10.5             # Numeric int_var <- 10L  #
Integer char_var <- "Hello"              #
Character log_var <- TRUE                    #
Logical
```

2.3 Assignment Operators

In R, you can assign values to variables using several assignment operators. The most common are:

`<-` (the preferred assignment operator)

`=` (also works for assignments)

`->` (assigns the value on the left to the variable on the right) ### Example:

```r
x <- 42  # Using the preferred assignment operator y = 10
      # Using the equals sign

15 -> z  # Assigning 15 to z
```

2.4 Basic Arithmetic Operations

R can perform various arithmetic operations, including addition, subtraction, multiplication, and division. Here's a breakdown of the primary arithmetic operators:

`+` for addition

`-` for subtraction

`*` for multiplication

`/` for division

`^` for exponentiation ### Example:

```r

a <- 5

b <- 3

addition <- a + b          # Result: 8 subtraction <- a - b          # Result: 2 multiplication <- a * b  # Result: 15 division <- a / b  #          Result:          1.6667 exponentiation <- a^b   # Result: 125

```

2.5 Data Structures in R

R offers several essential data structures to organize and manage data. The primary ones include: ### 2.5.1 Vectors

Vectors are one-dimensional arrays that can hold numeric, character, or logical data. They are created using the `c()` function.

```r

numeric_vector <- c(1, 2, 3, 4, 5)  char_vector <- c("apple", "banana", "cherry")

```

2.5.2 Matrices

Matrices are two-dimensional arrays that can store data in multiple rows and columns. They can be created using the `matrix()` function.

```r
matrix_data <- matrix(1:6, nrow = 2, ncol = 3)
```

2.5.3 Data Frames

Data frames are table-like structures that can contain different types of variables (numeric, character, etc.). They are crucial for data analysis.

```r
data_frame <- data.frame(
Name = c("Alice", "Bob", "Catherine"), Age = c(25, 30, 35),
Gender = c("F", "M", "F")
)
```

2.5.4 Lists

Lists can hold different types of objects, including vectors, other lists, or data frames. They are created using the `list()` function.

```r
my_list <- list(Name = "Alice", Age = 25, Scores = c(90, 85, 88))
```

24

2.6 Control Structures

Control structures are vital for directing the flow of your R program. The two most common control structures are `if` statements and loops.

2.6.1 If Statements

If statements allow you to execute certain code based on a condition.

```r
x <- 10
if (x > 5) {
print("x is greater than 5")
}
```

2.6.2 For Loops

For loops allow you to iterate over a sequence, such as a vector or a list.

```r
for (i in 1:5) { print(i)
}
```

2.7 Functions

Functions are reusable blocks of code that perform a specific task. You can use built-in functions or create your own.

Example of a Built-in Function:

```r
mean_value <- mean(c(1, 2, 3, 4, 5))  # Calculates the
mean of the vector

```

Example of a User-Defined Function:

```r
my_function <- function(x){ return(x^2)
}
result <- my_function(4) # Result: 16
```

Understanding basic R syntax is essential for harnessing the power of this versatile programming language. By familiarizing yourself with R's data types, structures, assignment operators, arithmetic operations, and control structures, you lay the groundwork for more advanced coding techniques and analysis.

Writing Your First R Script: Basic Commands and Operations

In this chapter, we will walk through the basic commands and operations that will form the foundation of your R programming skills. We'll cover how to set up your R environment, create and run your first script, and introduce basic commands for data manipulation and analysis.

Setting Up Your R Environment

Before diving into R scripting, it's essential to have the right tools set up. You'll need to install R and RStudio, a popular integrated development environment (IDE) for R that enhances productivity through an intuitive interface.

Install R: Download R from the Comprehensive R Archive Network (CRAN) at https://cran.r-project.org. Follow the installation instructions for your operating system.

Install RStudio: Go to the RStudio website at https://www.rstudio.com and download the free version of RStudio Desktop. Once installed, open RStudio and ensure it runs smoothly with your installed version of R.

Creating Your First R Script

After setting up your environment, you can create your first R script by following these steps:

Open RStudio: Launch the RStudio application.

Create a New Script: Click on `File` > `New File` > `R Script`. A new tab labeled "Untitled" will appear.

Save Your Script: Save your R script by clicking `File` > `Save` or using the shortcut `Ctrl + S` (Windows) or `Command + S` (Mac). Name your file with a `.R` extension, for example,

`my_first_script.R`.

Basic R Commands and Operations

Now that you have your R script ready, it's time to explore some basic commands and operations. ### 1. Comments

In R, comments are marked with the `#` symbol. This is useful for explaining your code or leaving notes for yourself or others.

```r
# This is a comment
# This line will not be executed
```

2. Assigning Values

You can store data in R using assignment operators like `<-` or `=`. The `<-` operator is traditionally favored in R for assignment.

```r
# Assigning a value to a variable x <- 5
y = 10
# Displaying the values x
y
```

3. Basic Arithmetic Operations

R can perform arithmetic operations just like a calculator. Here are some basic operations:

```r
# Basic arithmetic
sum <- x + y          # Addition difference <- y - x
            # Subtraction product <- x * y          #
```

Multiplication quotient <- y / x   # Division

Displaying the results sum

difference product quotient

```
```

4. Creating Vectors

Vectors are a fundamental data structure in R, which can store a sequence of data values. You can create a vector using the `c()` function:

```r
# Creating a vector my_vector <- c(1, 2, 3, 4, 5)
# Displaying the vector my_vector
```

5. Basic Functions

R is equipped with numerous built-in functions for data processing. You can use functions like `mean()`, `sum()`, and `length()` for basic operations.

```r
# Calculating mean and sum
mean_value <- mean(my_vector)  # Mean of the vector
sum_value <- sum(my_vector)    # Sum of the vector
# Displaying the results mean_value
sum_value
```

6. Control Structures

R supports control structures such as `if`, `for`, and `while`. Here is an example using a `for` loop:

```r
# A simple for loop for (i in my_vector) {

print(i)  # Prints each element of the vector

}
```

7. Installing and Loading Packages

R has a vibrant ecosystem of packages that extend its capabilities. You can install packages from CRAN using the `install.packages()` function and load them with `library()`.

```r
# Installing a package

install.packages("ggplot2") # Uncomment this line to run the installation

# Loading the package library(ggplot2)
```

8. Running Your Script

To execute the commands in your R script, you can highlight a section of code and press `Ctrl + Enter` (Windows) or `Command + Enter` (Mac). You can also run the entire script using the `Source` button in RStudio.

Practice these concepts to solidify your understanding. As you continue to explore R, you'll discover more advanced functions and techniques that will expand your analytical capabilities. In the following chapters, we will delve deeper into R's tools for data manipulation, visualization, and statistical analysis, setting the stage for your journey into the world of data science. Happy coding!

Variables and Assignment: Storing and Managing Data

This chapter will guide you through the essentials of variables in R, including how to create, use, and manipulate them, as well as their importance in data analysis.

1. What are Variables?

Variables can be thought of as containers for storing data values. In R, a variable can hold various types of data, including numbers, strings, vectors, matrices, lists, and data frames. Variables make it easier to refer to data by a name rather than a value, which enhances both readability and maintainability of your code.

1.1 Types of Variables

R supports several data types, each accommodating different kinds of information:

Numeric: Represents numbers, including integers and real numbers.

Character: Represents text or strings of characters.

Logical: Represents TRUE or FALSE values.

Factor: Represents categorical data and is used for statistical modeling.

Complex: Represents complex numbers. ### 1.2 Creating Variables

Creating a variable in R is straightforward. The assignment operator is used to assign a value to a variable. The most common assignment operators are `<-` (the preferred operator in R) and `=`.

Example:

```R

# Using the assignment operator (<-) x <- 10    # Numeric variable

name <- "John Doe"              # Character variable
is_active <- TRUE   # Logical variable
```

2. Assignment Operators

While the `<-` operator is the traditional assignment operator in R, R also supports the `=` operator for assignment, which can sometimes be more intuitive for those familiar with other programming languages.

2.1 Assignment Syntax

The basic syntax for variable assignment is:

```R
variable_name <- value
```
or

```R
variable_name = value
```

2.2 Best Practices

Though both operators can be used, the R community has a convention of preferring `<-` for general object assignment. This allows for visually clearer code and helps differentiate between assignments and function arguments, where `=` is commonly used.

3. Variable Naming Conventions

Choosing intuitive and meaningful variable names is crucial for code readability. Here are some common naming conventions:

Use descriptive names that reflect the content, e.g., `age`, `temperature`, `sales_data`.

Avoid using reserved words in R, such as `if`, `else`, `for`, `while`, and others.

Variable names should start with a letter and can contain letters, numbers, and underscores, but no spaces.

Example:

```R
# Good variable names total_sales <- 1500

client_list <- c("Alice", "Bob", "Charlie")

# Poor variable names

1st_variable <- 10    # Starts with a number (invalid)

data! <- "Sample"    # Contains special character (invalid)
```

4. Basic Operations with Variables

Once you have created variables, you can perform a variety

of operations. R supports arithmetic operations, logical operations, and vectorized operations which enable efficient data manipulation.

4.1 Arithmetic Operations

You can perform basic arithmetic operations like addition, subtraction, multiplication, and division directly on numeric variables:

```R
a <- 5
b <- 10

sum <- a + b  # Addition difference <- b - a  # Subtraction product <- a * b          # Multiplication quotient <- b / a     # Division
```

4.2 Using Variables in Functions

Variables play an important role in R's function-based environment. You can pass variables as arguments to functions for a variety of calculations:

```R
mean_value <- mean(c(a, b))  # Calculate the mean of a and b
```

5. Scope of Variables

The scope of a variable determines its visibility and lifetime. In R, variables can have different scopes:

Global Scope: Variables defined in the global environment can be accessed anywhere within your R session.

Local Scope: Variables defined within a function are local to that function and cannot be accessed outside it.

Understanding variable scope is important to avoid unintended consequences in your code. ### Example:

```R
my_function <- function() { local_var <- 10 # Local variable return(local_var)
}
my_function()       # Works fine
# print(local_var) # Error: object 'local_var' not found
```

6. Managing Variables

As data grows, managing variables effectively becomes essential. R provides various functions to help you inspect and manage the variables in your environment.

6.1 Listing Variables

You can use the `ls()` function to list all variables currently defined in your environment:

```R
ls() # Lists all variables
```

6.2 Removing Variables

To remove variables that are no longer needed, R offers

the `rm()` function:

```R
rm(x) # Removes the variable x from the environment
```

6.3 Checking Variable Type

The `class()` function allows you to check the type of a variable, which is helpful for debugging:

```R
class(name) # Returns "character" class(is_active) # Returns "logical"
```

Understanding how to effectively create and manage variables is crucial for any data analysis task or programming project. As you become more familiar with these concepts, you will find that efficiently managing your data and writing clean and readable R scripts becomes second nature.

Chapter 3: Data Types and Structures in R

At the core of any programming language are data types and data structures; understanding these is crucial for effective programming in R. In this chapter, we will explore the fundamental data types and structures available in R, their characteristics, and when to use them.

3.1 Basic Data Types in R

R primarily supports the following basic data types:

3.1.1 Numeric

The numeric type is used to represent numbers, including integers and floating-point numbers. In R, all numbers are treated as numeric by default. For instance, when you input `5` or `3.14`, R interprets them as numeric values.

```R
age <- 30      # Numeric value height <- 5.9            # Numeric value
```

3.1.2 Integer

While R automatically treats numbers as numeric, you can explicitly define an integer using the `L` suffix. This is particularly useful when dealing with large datasets or for memory optimization.

```R
num_integer <- 5L  # Integer type
```

3.1.3 Character

Character values are used to store text data. Character vectors are created using quotes, either single or double. In R, any non-numeric element is treated as a character.

```R
name <- "Alice"      # Character type
message <- 'Welcome to R!' # Character type
```

3.1.4 Logical

Logical data types represent boolean values: `TRUE` or `FALSE`. These are often used in conditional statements and can be the result of comparisons.

```R
is_active <- TRUE   # Logical type
is_adult <- age >= 18  # Logical type based on comparison
```

3.1.5 Complex

Complex data types consist of real and imaginary parts, represented as `a + bi`, where `i` is the imaginary unit. Each complex number is created using the `complex` function or by adding a real and imaginary component.

```R
z <- 2 + 3i  # Complex type
```

3.2 Data Structures in R

R offers several data structures to organize and manipulate data. Understanding these structures is crucial for efficient data analysis.

3.2.1 Vectors

A vector is the most basic data structure in R and can hold multiple elements of the same type. They are created using the `c()` function (concatenate).

```R
numeric_vector <- c(1, 2, 3, 4) character_vector <- c("red", "green", "blue") logical_vector <- c(TRUE, FALSE, TRUE)

# Accessing vector elements

first_element <- numeric_vector[1]  # Retrieves the first element, which is 1
```

3.2.2 Matrices

Matrices are two-dimensional arrays that can hold elements of the same type. They are created using the

`matrix()` function, where you specify the number of rows and columns.

```R
my_matrix <- matrix(1:9, nrow=3, ncol=3)
```

3.2.3 Arrays

Like matrices, arrays are multi-dimensional structures

capable of holding elements of the same type. The `array()` function creates an array.

```R
my_array <- array(1:12, dim = c(2, 3, 2))  # A 2x3x2 array
```

3.2.4 Lists

Lists are versatile data structures that can hold different types and sizes of data. They are created using the `list()` function and can include vectors, matrices, data frames, and even other lists.

```R
my_list <- list(name="Alice", age=30, scores=c(90, 85, 88))
```

3.2.5 Data Frames

Data frames are tabular data structures that allow you to store data in rows and columns. Each column can contain different data types—making them similar to tables in a database or spreadsheets. Data frames can be created using the `data.frame()` function.

```R
my_data_frame <- data.frame(Name=c("Alice", "Bob"),
Age=c(30, 25),
Height=c(5.5, 6.0))
```

```
```

3.2.6 Factors

Factors are used to handle categorical data, which is essential in statistical modeling and analysis. They help R to treat categorical variables appropriately. You can create a factor with the `factor()` function.

```R
gender <- factor(c("Male", "Female", "Female", "Male"), levels=c("Male", "Female"))
```

3.3 Understanding Data Manipulation

Once you grasp the data types and structures, understanding how to manipulate and transform these structures is essential. R offers various functions and packages for data manipulation, including `dplyr` for data frames. With these tools, you can filter, select, mutate, and summarize your data efficiently.

3.3.1 Common Functions for Data Manipulation

`str()`: Displays the structure of an object.

`summary()`: Provides a summary of the object, including statistics for numerical data and counts for categorical data.

`head()` and `tail()`: Show the first or last few elements of an object.

`length()`: Returns the number of elements in a vector or the number of rows in a data frame.

```R
```

```
# Example of using summary and head
summary(my_data_frame) head(my_data_frame)
```

Understanding these components is foundational for data analysis and programming in R. As you progress in your R journey, mastering these types and structures will empower you to manipulate and analyze data effectively, paving the way for more advanced topics in R programming.

Vectors, Lists, and Matrices: The Building Blocks of R

This chapter delves into three essential building blocks of R: vectors, lists, and matrices. Understanding these structures provides a foundation for effective data manipulation and analysis, making it easier to work with complex datasets.

Vectors: The Backbone of R

At the core of R's data handling capabilities is the vector, a one-dimensional array that can store elements of the same type (numeric, character, logical, etc.). Vectors are fundamental in R because they provide a simple way to store and operate on data.

Creating Vectors

Vectors in R can be created using the `c()` function, which stands for "concatenate". For example:

```R
numeric_vector <- c(1, 2, 3, 4, 5) character_vector <-
```

c("a", "b", "c") logical_vector <- c(TRUE, FALSE, TRUE)
```

Vectors can also be generated using functions like `seq()` for sequences and `rep()` for repetition. ### Accessing Elements

Elements within a vector can be accessed using square brackets `[ ]`. Indices in R are 1-based, meaning the first element has an index of 1:

```R

first_element <- numeric_vector[1] # Returns 1
```

Vector Operations

R supports vectorized operations, which means you can perform arithmetic operations on entire vectors without needing for loops. This feature allows for concise and efficient code:

```R

squared_vector <- numeric_vector^2 # Returns c(1, 4, 9, 16, 25)
```

Broadcasting rules apply, enabling R to perform operations even when vectors are of different lengths, enhancing computational efficiency.

Lists: The Flexible Containers

While vectors are great for storing homogeneous data, lists provide a flexible container that can hold elements of different types and lengths. This characteristic makes lists
```

particularly useful when handling complex data structures.
Creating Lists

Lists can be created using the `list()` function. For instance:

```R
my_list <- list(name = "John", age = 30, scores = c(90, 80, 85))
```

Here, `my_list` contains a character string, an integer, and a numeric vector, showcasing the versatility of lists.

Accessing Elements

You can access list elements using double square brackets `[[ ]]` for extracting elements and the `$` operator for named components:

```R
age <- my_list[[2]]  # Returns 30

name <- my_list$name    # Returns "John"
```

Nesting Lists

Lists can also contain other lists, allowing for hierarchical data storage. For example, consider a list of students, where each student's information is stored in a separate list:

```R
students <- list(

student1 = list(name = "Alice", age = 22), student2 =
```

```
list(name = "Bob", age = 24)
)
```
```

```

This capability makes lists ideal for structured data like JSON or XML formats. ## Matrices: The Two-Dimensional Data Structure

Matrices are two-dimensional arrays that require all elements to be of the same data type. They are particularly useful for mathematical computations and operations involving data that is best represented in a grid format.

Creating Matrices

Matrices can be constructed using the `matrix()` function. For example:

```R
my_matrix <- matrix(1:9, nrow = 3, ncol = 3)
```

This creates a 3x3 matrix filled with numbers from 1 to 9, filled by column by default. ### Accessing Elements

Similar to vectors, elements in a matrix are accessed using square brackets, but with the addition of specifying the row and column indexes:

```R
element <- my_matrix[2, 3] # Returns 6
```

Matrix Operations

Matrices support various operations such as addition, subtraction, multiplication, and transposition. R's built-in functions and operators enable matrix manipulation with ease:

```R
transposed_matrix <- t(my_matrix)      # Transposes the matrix
```

Matrix multiplication can be performed using the `%*%` operator, allowing for linear algebra operations crucial in statistical modeling and machine learning.

Vectors, lists, and matrices form the backbone of data manipulation in R. Each data structure serves a unique purpose, making R a flexible tool for a diverse range of applications from simple calculations to complex statistical analyses.

Data Frames and Tibbles: Working with Tabular Data

In R, one of the most common ways to organize data is through tabular structures, primarily using data frames and tibbles. Understanding how to create, manipulate, and analyze these data structures is essential for any data scientist or analyst. This chapter delves into data frames and tibbles, exploring their characteristics, differences, and best practices for effective data manipulation in R.

1. Understanding Data Frames ### 1.1 What is a Data Frame?

A data frame in R is a table-like structure that stores data in a two-dimensional format. Each column can contain different types of data—numeric, character, factor, etc.— while each row typically represents an observation or record. You can think of a data frame as a collection of vectors of equal length, where each vector corresponds to a column.

1.2 Creating a Data Frame

You can create a data frame using the `data.frame()` function. Here's a simple example:

```R
# Create vectors for each column names <- c("Alice", "Bob", "Charlie") ages <- c(25, 30, 35)

height <- c(5.5, 6.0, 5.8)

# Combine into a data frame

df <- data.frame(Name = names, Age = ages, Height = height)

# Print the data frame print(df)
```

1.3 Accessing Data in Data Frames

Data frames allow for versatile access to data. You can access specific columns, rows, and individual elements using a variety of methods:

- **Column Access**: Use the `$` operator or double square brackets `[[ ]]` to access a specific column.

```R
```

```R
# Access the 'Age' column ages_vector <- df$Age
print(ages_vector)
```

- **Row Access**: Use the square brackets to access particular rows.

```R
# Access the first row first_row <- df[1, ] print(first_row)
```

- **Element Access**: To retrieve a specific element, you can specify both row and column indices.

```R
# Access the element at the second row, third column element <- df[2, 3]

print(element)
```

1.4 Modifying Data Frames

You can modify existing data frames by adding or deleting columns and rows, or by altering the contents of specific cells.

```R
# Adding a new column

df$Weight <- c(130, 180, 150) # Adding weights print(df)

# Modifying an existing value df[1, "Age"] <- 26

print(df)
```

```
# Deleting a column df$Weight <- NULL print(df)
```

2. Introduction to Tibbles ### 2.1 What is a Tibble?

A tibble is a modern reimagining of the data frame, introduced as part of the tidyverse package in R. Tibbles contain similar features to data frames but come with some enhanced functionalities, primarily focused on usability and readability. They make it easier to work with data by maintaining a clearer structure and preventing common pitfalls that can occur with traditional data frames.

2.2 Creating a Tibble

You can create a tibble using the `tibble()` function from the `tibble` package. Here's how you can create a tibble:

```R
# Creating a tibble library(tibble)
```

```
tbl <- tibble(Name = names, Age = ages, Height = height) print(tbl)
```

2.3 Key Differences between Data Frames and Tibbles

Printing: Tibbles print only the first 10 rows and the columns that fit on the screen, while data frames will print the entire content to the console.

Data Types: Tibbles are less strict about the types of

49

columns and will retain the type of the data you provide without converting it to a more generic type.

Subsetting: When using `[[ ]]` on a tibble, it returns a vector, whereas the same operation on a data frame returns a subset of the data frame.

2.4 Manipulating Tibbles

Working with tibbles is similar to working with data frames, but it integrates seamlessly with the tidyverse, allowing you to leverage functions from packages like `dplyr` for data manipulation.

```R
library(dplyr)

# Selecting columns with dplyr selected_tbl <- tbl %>% select(Name, Age) print(selected_tbl)

# Filtering rows

filtered_tbl <- tbl %>% filter(Age > 28) print(filtered_tbl)
```

3. Best Practices for Using Data Frames and Tibbles

Choose the Right Structure: If you're working with a simple dataset or need compatibility with base R functions, data frames are appropriate. For modern data analysis, especially within the tidyverse framework, tibbles are generally preferred.

Naming Conventions: Use descriptive and consistent naming for columns to improve readability and maintainability.

Data Cleaning: Always inspect and clean your data before analysis. Functions like `head()`, `summary()`, and `glimpse()` (for tibbles) can help evaluate the dataset quickly.

Use dplyr for Manipulation: Leverage the `dplyr` package for efficient data manipulation. Its chaining and readability can significantly enhance productivity.

Stay Updated: R and its libraries are continually evolving. Regularly updating your packages can help you utilize the latest features and improvements.

We've explored the foundational elements of working with tabular data in R through data frames and tibbles. Understanding their structures, advantages, and methods of manipulation is vital for effective data analysis. By applying these concepts, you'll be well-equipped to handle, analyze, and visualize data efficiently, paving the way for insightful analysis and informed decision-making in your data projects.

Chapter 4: Control Structures and Logical Operations

In this chapter, we will delve into the various control structures available in R, including conditionals and loops, as well as the logical operations that allow for decision-making based on specific conditions.

4.1 Introduction to Control Structures

Control structures govern the flow of execution in a program. They dictate how statements are executed based on certain conditions or how often certain blocks of code are run. The two primary types of control structures in R are:

Conditional statements (if, else)

Loops (for, while, repeat)

These structures help in making decisions, executing specific blocks of code under particular conditions, and iterating over data.

4.1.1 Conditional Statements

Conditional statements allow the programmer to execute certain code only if a condition is met. The basic syntax for an `if` statement in R is as follows:

```r
if (condition) {
# Code to execute if condition is TRUE
}
```

You can also include an `else` clause, which executes if the condition is FALSE:

```r
if (condition) {
# Code to execute if condition is TRUE
} else {
# Code to execute if condition is FALSE
}
```

For multiple conditions, the `else if` construct can be used:

```r
if (condition1) {
# Code for condition1
} else if (condition2) { # Code for condition2
} else {
# Code if no conditions are met
}
```

Example of Conditional Statements

Let's consider a simple example where we check if a number is positive, negative, or zero.

```r
number <- -5
```

```r
if (number > 0) {
print("The number is positive.")
} else if (number < 0) { print("The number is negative.")
} else {
print("The number is zero.")
}
```

4.1.2 Logical Operations

Logical operations are essential in manipulating Boolean values (TRUE or FALSE). In R, you can use logical operators such as:

- `&` (and)
- `|` (or)
- `!` (not)

These operations allow for more complex conditions to be evaluated. #### Example of Logical Operations

```r
x <- 5
y <- 10
if (x > 0 & y > 0) {
print("Both x and y are positive.")
}
```

4.2 Looping Constructs

In addition to conditionals, loops allow us to execute a block of code multiple times. R provides several looping constructs:

For Loops

While Loops

Repeat Loops #### 4.2.1 For Loops

A `for` loop is typically used when the number of iterations is known beforehand. The syntax is:

```r
for (variable in sequence) { # Code to execute
}
```

Example of For Loops

Suppose we want to print the squares of the first five integers:

```r
for (i in 1:5) { print(i^2)
}
```

4.2.2 While Loops

A `while` loop continues to execute as long as a specified condition is TRUE. Its syntax looks like this:

```r
while (condition) { # Code to execute
```

```
}
```

Example of While Loops

Here's an example where we use a while loop to count down from 5 to 1:

```r
count <- 5

while (count > 0) { print(count)  count <- count - 1

}
```

4.2.3 Repeat Loops

A `repeat` loop is similar to a while loop, but it does not have a specified condition. Instead, the loop continues indefinitely until it is explicitly broken out of with a break statement.

```r repeat {

# Code to execute if (condition) {

break

}

}
```

Example of Repeat Loops

We can use a repeat loop to continue counting until a specific condition is met.

```r
```

```r
count <- 1

repeat { print(count)
count <- count + 1 if (count > 5) {
break
}
}
```

4.3 Combining Control Structures

Often, you will need to use control structures in conjunction in a single application. Here is a simple example combining loops and conditionals to sum even numbers from 1 to 10:

```r
sum_even <- 0 for (i in 1:10) {

if (i %% 2 == 0) {  # Check if the number is even
sum_even <- sum_even + i

}
}
print(sum_even)
```

In this chapter, we explored control structures and logical operations in R programming, focusing on conditionals and loops, which provide the fundamental building blocks for decision-making in code. By understanding and applying these concepts, you can write more robust and dynamic R scripts that can handle complex operations effectively.

Conditional Statements (if-else) and Loops (for, while)

These tools enable you to make decisions and perform repetitive tasks efficiently, which is essential for complex data manipulation and analysis. In this chapter, we will explore how to use conditional statements (`if`, `else`) and loops (`for`, `while`) in R, providing practical examples and explaining their syntax and best practices.

Conditional Statements

Conditional statements in R allow you to execute different code based on whether a given condition is true or false. The most common form of a conditional statement is the `if-else` statement.

The `if` Statement

The basic syntax for the `if` statement is as follows:

```R
if (condition) {

# code to execute if the condition is true

}
```

Example:

```R
```

```R
x <- 15
if (x > 10) {
print("x is greater than 10")
}
```

In this example, the message "x is greater than 10" will be printed because the condition (`x > 10`) evaluates to true.

The `if-else` Statement

The `if-else` statement allows you to specify an alternative code block that executes when the condition is false:

```R
if (condition) {
# code to execute if the condition is true
} else {
# code to execute if the condition is false
}
```

Example:

```R
x <- 5
if (x > 10) {
print("x is greater than 10")
} else {
print("x is 10 or less")
```

```
}
```
```

```

This example prints "x is 10 or less" because the condition is false. ### The `ifelse` Function

R also provides a vectorized version of the `if` statement called `ifelse()`. It is particularly useful for applying a condition across whole vectors.

Syntax:

```R
ifelse(test, yes, no)
```

Example:

```R
scores <- c(85, 60, 75, 90)
result <- ifelse(scores >= 75, "Pass", "Fail") print(result)
```

In this case, the `result` vector will contain "Pass" or "Fail" based on the scores evaluated. ## Loops

Loops are used to execute a block of code multiple times, which can significantly simplify repetitive tasks. R provides several types of loops, but the two most commonly used are `for` loops and `while` loops.

The `for` Loop

The `for` loop iterates over a sequence (like a vector or a list) and executes a block of code for each element.

Syntax:

```R
for (variable in sequence) { # code to execute
}
```

Example:

```R
numbers <- 1:5

for (num in numbers) { print(num^2)
}
```

The above loop prints the square of each number from 1 to 5. ### The `while` Loop

A `while` loop continues to execute as long as a specified condition is true.

Syntax:

```R
while (condition) { # code to execute
}
```

Example:

```R
count <- 1
while (count <= 5) { print(count)
count <- count + 1
```

```
}
```
```

```

This loop will print numbers 1 to 5. It demonstrates how to control the loop's iteration by manually adjusting a variable (`count`).

Nested Conditional Statements and Loops

You can nest `if-else` statements and loops within each other to create more complex logic. However, excessive nesting may lead to code that is difficult to read and maintain, so it's essential to maintain clarity.

Example of Nested `if` Statements:

```R
x <- 15
if (x > 10) {
if (x > 20) {
print("x is greater than 20")
} else {
print("x is greater than 10 but less than or equal to 20")
}
}
```

Example of Nested Loops:

```R
for (i in 1:3) {
```

```
for (j in 1:2) {
print(paste("i =", i, "j =", j))
}
}
```
` ` `

The outer loop iterates through 1 to 3 while the inner loop runs through 1 to 2 for each iteration of the outer loop, resulting in a combination of outputs.

Best Practices

Comment Your Code: Use comments to explain complex logic in your conditional statements and loops. This practice makes your code more understandable to others (and to yourself, later on).

Avoid Deep Nesting: Aim to keep nested statements manageable. Consider refactoring your code into functions if it becomes too complex.

Use Vectorization: Whenever possible, leverage R's vectorized operations, which are often faster and more efficient than writing loops.

Preallocate Memory: When using loops to build up a vector or data structure, preallocate memory for better performance.

Conditional statements and loops are essential tools in R that enable you to control the flow of your programs and automate repetitive tasks effectively. This chapter explored the syntax and application of `if`,

`else`, `for`, and `while` constructs.

Logical Operators and Expressions: Making Decisions in R

Understanding how to use these tools effectively is crucial for creating robust and efficient R programs. In this chapter, we will explore the various logical operators available in R, how to construct logical expressions, and how to utilize these components to make decisions in our code.

4.1 Introduction to Logical Operators

Logical operators perform logical operations on one or more boolean values (TRUE or FALSE) and are integral to formulating logical expressions. In R, there are three primary logical operators:

AND (`&` and `&&`):

The `&` operator performs element-wise logical AND. It evaluates both sides of the expression for every element in a vector.

The `&&` operator is a more efficient version that evaluates the right side only if the left side is TRUE. It is typically used with single logical conditions rather than vectors.

OR (`|` and `||`):

The `|` operator performs element-wise logical OR.

The `||` operator behaves similarly to `&&`, only evaluating the right side if the left side is FALSE, and is suitable for single logical expressions.

NOT (`!`):

The `!` operator negates a boolean value, turning TRUE to FALSE and vice versa.

Example

```r
x <- TRUE y <- FALSE
# AND
result_and <- x & y # FALSE
# OR
result_or <- x | y  # TRUE
# NOT
result_not <- !x     # FALSE
```

4.2 Logical Expressions

Logical expressions are combinations of logical operators and variables that evaluate to a boolean value (TRUE or FALSE). These expressions are fundamental to controlling program flow, including conditionals and loops.

Comparison Operators

Before diving into logical expressions, it's essential to understand comparison operators, which compare two values and return a boolean result. Some common comparison operators in R include:

`==`: Equals

`!=`: Not equal

`` ` `>`: Greater than

`<`: Less than

`>=`: Greater than or equal to

`<=`: Less than or equal to

Creating Logical Expressions

You can create logical expressions by combining these comparison operators with logical operators. For instance:

```r
a <- 5

b <- 10

expression_1 <- a < b      # TRUE expression_2 <- a == 5 && b > 5    # TRUE expression_3 <- !(a >= b)
     # TRUE
```

In these examples, the logical expressions evaluate to boolean values based on the conditions set by the comparisons.

4.3 Conditional Statements

Conditional statements, such as `if`, `else if`, and `else`, are vital for controlling the flow of execution in R based on logical expressions. They allow you to execute specific code blocks when conditions are met.

Basic `if` Statement

The simplest form is the `if` statement, which executes a block of code if a condition evaluates to TRUE.

```r
```

```r
x <- 10
if (x > 5) {
print("x is greater than 5")
}
```

`if-else` Statement

To cover multiple scenarios, you can use an `if-else` statement. If the condition in the `if` statement evaluates to FALSE, the code inside the `else` block is executed.

```r
x <- 4
if (x > 5) {
print("x is greater than 5")
} else {
print("x is 5 or less")
}
```

`else if` Statement

When more than two possible outcomes are required, you can chain multiple `else if` statements.

```r
x <- 7
if (x < 5) {
```

```r
print("x is less than 5")
} else if (x >= 5 && x <= 10) { print("x is between 5 and 10")
} else {
print("x is greater than 10")
}
```

4.4 The `switch` Statement

For scenarios where multiple choices must be evaluated based on a single expression, the `switch` statement is a convenient alternative to numerous `if-else` constructs. It evaluates its first argument and returns the corresponding code block associated with that value.

```r
day <- "Monday"
switch(day,
"Monday" = print("Start of the week!"), "Friday" = print("Almost weekend!"), "Saturday" = print("Weekend!"), "Sunday" = print("Rest day!"), print("Midweek day"))
```

4.5 Control Structures with Loops

While logical operators and expressions shine in conditional statements, they are also essential for controlling loops. R provides several types of loops such as `for`, `while`, and `repeat`, where logical conditions determine how many times the loop executes.

Example of a `while` Loop

A `while` loop continues as long as a specified condition is TRUE.

```r
count <- 1

while (count <= 5) { print(count)

count <- count + 1

}
```

4.6 Practice Exercises

To reinforce your understanding of logical operators and expressions, try out the following exercises:

Write a program that checks whether a number is positive, negative, or zero using conditional statements.

Use the `switch` statement to create a simple menu that responds to user choices.

Create a loop that sums numbers from a vector until the sum exceeds 100 and then prints the final sum.

We delved into the world of logical operators and expressions in R, exploring how they facilitate decision-making in programming. From understanding comparison and logical operators to controlling program flow with conditional statements and loops, you now possess the tools to make your R programs dynamic and responsive to different conditions.

Chapter 5: Functions and Modularity in R

In R, functions enable users to encapsulate code for specific tasks, allowing for modular programming paradigms. This chapter will explore the concept of functions in R, focusing on their definition, utilization, and the principles of modularity that enhance code organization and efficiency.

5.1 Understanding Functions in R

A function in R is a set of statements structured to perform a specific task. Functions can take inputs (arguments), process data, and return output values. By defining functions, users can streamline their code and avoid redundancy, thereby fostering cleaner and more efficient analysis.

5.1.1 Defining a Function

To define a function in R, the `function` keyword is employed. The basic structure is as follows:

```R
function_name <- function(arg1, arg2, ...) { # Code to execute

return(result)

}
```

Let's illustrate this with a simple example:

```R
add_numbers <- function(x, y) { result <- x + y
```

```
return(result)

}
```

Here, `add_numbers` is a function that takes two arguments, `x` and `y`, and returns their sum. This simple encapsulation of the addition operation can be reused any number of times simply by calling

`add_numbers(3, 5)`.

5.1.2 Function Arguments

Functions in R can accept various types of arguments. These can be positional, named, or even default arguments.

Positional Arguments: Required to be passed in order.

Named Arguments: Can be passed in any order by using their names.

Default Arguments: Allow a function to be called with fewer arguments than defined. Here's an example with default arguments:

```R
greet <- function(name, greeting = "Hello") { message <-
paste(greeting, name) return(message)


}
print(greet("Alice"))#    Outputs:    "Hello    Alice"
print(greet("Bob", "Hi"))        # Outputs: "Hi Bob"
```

5.2 Scope of Variables

Understanding the scope of variables within a function is crucial for proper function design. Variables defined inside a function are said to have local scope and cannot be accessed outside the function.

Conversely, global variables are accessible from anywhere in the R environment.

```R
glo_var <- "I am global"

my_function <- function() { loc_var <- "I am local"
return(loc_var)

}

print(my_function())              # Outputs: "I am local"
print(glo_var)       # Outputs: "I am global"

# print(loc_var)    # Throws an error, loc_var is not found
```

This distinction enhances modularity, as functions do not inadvertently modify global state, allowing for safer and easier debugging.

5.3 Returning Values

Functions can return multiple values by returning a list. This can be particularly useful when multiple outputs are required from a single function.

```R
calculate_statistics <- function(data) { mean_value <- mean(data) median_value <- median(data)
```

```
return(list(mean  =  mean_value,  median  =
median_value))
}
stats  <-  calculate_statistics(c(1,  2,  3,  4,  5))
print(stats$mean)  # Outputs: 3 print(stats$median)  #
Outputs: 3
```
```

## 5.4 Modularity in R Programming

Modularity involves breaking down a complex task into smaller, manageable functions. This methodological approach not only enhances readability but also facilitates testing and debugging.

### 5.4.1 Benefits of Modularity

**Reusability**: Functions can be reused across different scripts and projects. If a good function is written once, there's no need to rewrite it.

**Testing**: Smaller, self-contained functions are analogous to test units. They can be tested independently, simplifying the debugging process.

**Collaboration**: In team settings, modular code enables easier collaboration as team members can work on different functions without interfering with one another's code.

### 5.4.2 Organizing Code with Functions

Organizing the analysis workflow as a series of modular functions can greatly improve the development process. Consider the following example in the context of data analysis:
```

```R
load_data    <-    function(file_path)    {    data    <-
read.csv(file_path) return(data)

}

clean_data    <-    function(data)    {    cleaned_data    <-
na.omit(data) return(cleaned_data)

}

analyze_data <- function(data) { result <- summary(data)
return(result)

}

file_path <- "data.csv"

data    <-    load_data(file_path)    cleaned_data    <-
clean_data(data)

analysis_result <- analyze_data(cleaned_data)
```

In this example, each function serves a distinct role in the data processing pipeline. This clear separation of concerns enhances code clarity and allows for easier adjustments in one portion of the code without impacting others.

By leveraging functions, users can create organized, reusable, and maintainable code structures, promoting better practices in data analysis and computational tasks.

Creating and Using Functions: The Power of Reusability

This chapter explores the fundamentals of creating and using functions in R, emphasizing their importance in promoting code reusability and efficiency.

1. Understanding Functions in R

A function in R is a set of instructions organized into a block of code that can be executed anytime by invoking its name. Functions allow you to perform specific tasks without rewriting code, making your scripts cleaner and easier to maintain.

1.1 Anatomy of a Function

The general syntax for creating a function in R is as follows:

```R
function_name <- function(arg1, arg2, ...) { # Code to execute

return(value)

}
```

function_name: The name you give to the function. It's essential for readability and should be descriptive of what the function does.

arg1, arg2, ...: These are the arguments the function accepts. They are inputs that allow users to customize the function's behavior.

return(value): This optional statement specifies what the function will return after execution. ### 1.2 Example of a Simple Function

Let's create a simple function that calculates the area of a rectangle:

```R
calculate_area <- function(length, width) { area <- length * width

return(area)

}
```

To use this function, you would call it with specific values for length and width:

```R
result <- calculate_area(5, 10) print(result) # Outputs 50
```

2. Benefits of Using Functions ### 2.1 Code Reusability

The primary advantage of functions is reusability. Once defined, a function can be used multiple times throughout your script or even in different scripts. This significantly reduces redundancy and the potential for errors.

2.2 Improved Readability

Functions can make your code easier to understand. By breaking down complex tasks into smaller, manageable pieces, you can improve the readability of your code, making it easier for others (and yourself) to navigate in the future.

76

2.3 Easier Debugging

When you encapsulate code into functions, it becomes easier to isolate and identify errors. If a function isn't returning the expected result, you know exactly where to look instead of sifting through a lengthy script.

3. Passing Arguments ### 3.1 Default Arguments

You can assign default values to arguments in a function. This means that if no value is provided when the function is called, the default will be used.

```R
calculate_area <- function(length, width = 1) { area <- length * width

return(area)

}

print(calculate_area(5)) # Outputs 5 (default width of 1)
```

3.2 Variable Number of Arguments

R allows for functions to accept a variable number of arguments using the `...` syntax. This is useful when you don't know beforehand how many arguments will be passed.

```R
summarize_values <- function(...) { values <- c(...)

return(sum(values))

}

print(summarize_values(1, 2, 3, 4, 5)) # Outputs 15
```

```
```

4. Returning Values

Functions can return multiple values using lists. This is particularly handy when a task requires generating more than one output.

```R
calculate_statistics <- function(x) { mean_value <- mean(x)

sd_value <- sd(x)

return(list(mean = mean_value, sd = sd_value))


}

stats <- calculate_statistics(c(1, 2, 3, 4, 5)) print(stats$mean) # Outputs 3 print(stats$sd) # Outputs 1.581139
```

5. Best Practices for Function Creation

While creating functions in R, adhere to the following best practices to ensure clarity, consistency, and maintainability:

5.1 Meaningful Names

Choose names that reflect the function's purpose. Avoid vague titles like `function1` or `doSomething`. ### 5.2 Document Your Functions

Use comments, and document your functions with the `roxygen2` package to explain inputs, outputs, and any side effects.

5.3 Keep Functions Focused

Design functions to perform a single task. A focused function is easier to understand, test, and reuse. ### 5.4 Test Thoroughly

Before utilizing functions in critical analysis, test them with various inputs, including edge cases and invalid data.

6. Advanced Function Techniques ### 6.1 Anonymous Functions

Sometimes, you might require a temporary function that you don't intend to reuse elsewhere. In such cases, anonymous functions can be used with the `lapply()` or `sapply()` functions.

```R
result <- sapply(1:5, function(x) x^2) print(result)  # Outputs the squares of 1 to 5
```

6.2 Nested Functions

Functions can call other functions, leading to more modular code design. However, it's crucial to ensure that nested functions remain clear and manageable.

```R
outer_function <- function(a) { inner_function <- function(b) { return(a + b)
}
return(inner_function(5))
```

```
}
```

```
print(outer_function(10)) # Outputs 15
```
```
` ` `
```

By mastering the art of function creation, R programmers can significantly elevate their coding practices, making their analyses more robust and easier to manage. As you continue your journey in R programming, consider functions not just as tools but as essential building blocks of your code that will save you time and effort in the long run.

Built-in Functions vs. Custom Functions: When to Use What

With its extensive library of built-in functions, R allows users to perform a myriad of tasks efficiently without needing to code from scratch. However, as projects grow in complexity, there often comes a point when relying solely on built-in functions may not be sufficient. This chapter examines the differences between built-in functions and custom functions, along with practical guidelines on when to use each type in R programming.

Understanding Built-in Functions ### Definition and Examples

Built-in functions are pre-defined functions available in R and its libraries. These functions are designed for various tasks, such as statistical calculations, data manipulation, and graphical representation. Some common examples include:

`mean()`: Computes the average of a numeric vector.

`lm()`: Fits linear models.

`summary()`: Provides a summary of statistical models or data frames.

`ggplot()`: Used to create visualizations using the grammar of graphics. ### Advantages of Built-in Functions

Efficiency: Built-in functions are optimized for performance, making them faster and more efficient than custom implementations.

Reliability: Being part of a robust programming environment, built-in functions have been extensively tested and accepted in the statistical community.

Ease of Use: They come with comprehensive documentation, making it easier for users to get help and understand their usage.

Simplicity: Many built-in functions can perform complex tasks with just a single line of code, making it simpler to write and read R code.

Disadvantages of Built-in Functions

Limited Flexibility: Built-in functions may not accommodate unique needs or complex requirements of specific projects.

Less Customization: Users have less control over the internal workings of built-in functions, which may result in unsatisfactory outputs according to specific parameters.

Understanding Custom Functions ### Definition and

Examples

Custom functions are user-defined functions created to meet specific needs of a particular project or analysis. They are defined using the `function` keyword in R, allowing programmers to encapsulate code into reusable blocks.

Example of a custom function:

```r
# A custom function to calculate the variance
custom_variance <- function(x) {

n <- length(x) mean_x <- mean(x)

return(sum((x - mean_x)^2) / (n - 1))

}
```

Advantages of Custom Functions

Flexibility: Custom functions allow for the implementation of specific logic and procedures tailored to the needs of a project.

Reusability: Once defined, custom functions can be reused throughout the code, significantly reducing redundancy.

Clarity: They can make the code more readable if well-named, as the function name can describe its purpose.

Customization: Users can control calculations and outputs, allowing for unique analyses that go beyond what built-in functions can offer.

Disadvantages of Custom Functions

Performance: Custom functions are often less optimized than built-in functions, especially if not written efficiently.

Development Time: Writing custom functions requires additional time and effort, particularly for complex analyses that could be accomplished with simpler built-in functions.

Potential Errors: Custom functions are developed by the user and might contain errors or bugs that could lead to incorrect results if not adequately tested.

When to Use Built-in Functions

Built-in functions are particularly useful when:

Performing Standard Operations: If the task is a common statistical analysis or data manipulation that is easily handled by existing functions, such as calculating a mean or generating a summary of a dataset.

Rapid Prototyping: In the early stages of a project, speed is essential, and leveraging built-in functions can help prototype ideas quickly.

Collaborative Projects: When working with teammates or stakeholders, using standard functions ensures that others can easily understand and replicate the analysis.

When to Use Custom Functions

Custom functions should be considered when:

Complex Analysis: If the analysis requires steps that

are not adequately addressed by built-in functions, custom functions may be needed to encapsulate this complexity.

Repetitive Tasks: For repeated calculations or processes throughout an analysis, defining a custom function can make the code more concise and manageable.

Unique Requirements: When working with specialized datasets or methodologies that cannot be fully captured by existing functions, creating a custom function allows for complete control over the logic.

Testing and Debugging: When developing new methods, custom functions allow for a focused environment to validate algorithms and logic independently.

By understanding the strengths and limitations of each type of function, you can make informed decisions about when to leverage existing tools and when to extend your programming capabilities with custom solutions. This strategic approach will not only enhance your efficiency but also contribute to the overall quality of your data analysis projects in R.

Chapter 6: Data Importing and Exporting

This chapter will explore the various methods of importing data into R from different sources, as well as how to export data from R into various formats for further analysis or reporting.

6.1 Introduction to Data Importing and Exporting

Before diving into specific methods, it's essential to understand the importance of data importing and exporting. In R programming, importing refers to bringing external data into the R environment for analysis, while exporting involves saving processed or analyzed data from R to external files.

The ability to import and export data effectively allows analysts to leverage the power of R in combination with other tools and platforms. This chapter focuses on common data formats such as CSV, Excel, JSON, and databases, as well as techniques for handling these formats.

6.2 Importing Data

6.2.1 Importing CSV Files

One of the most common formats for data exchange is the Comma-Separated Values (CSV) file. R provides the `read.csv()` function for importing CSV files. Here's how to use it:

```R
# Importing a CSV file

data <- read.csv("path/to/your/file.csv", header = TRUE,
```

```
sep = ",")
```
```

```

`header = TRUE` indicates that the first row contains column names.

`sep = ","` defines the delimiter (comma in this case).

For larger datasets, the `fread()` function from the `data.table` package is often preferred for its speed:

```R
library(data.table)

data <- fread("path/to/your/file.csv")
```

6.2.2 Importing Excel Files

Excel spreadsheets are another popular format for data storage. The `readxl` package provides a straightforward way to read Excel files. Here is an example:

```R
library(readxl)

# Reading an Excel file

data <- read_excel("path/to/your/file.xlsx", sheet = 1)
```

The `sheet` argument specifies which sheet to import.
6.2.3 Importing JSON Files

JSON (JavaScript Object Notation) format is commonly used for data interchange. The `jsonlite` package makes it easy to read JSON files:

```R
library(jsonlite)

# Importing JSON data
```

```R
data <- fromJSON("path/to/your/file.json")
```

6.2.4 Importing Data from Databases

R can connect to various databases using packages such as `DBI` and `RSQLite`. The following example shows how to import data from a SQLite database:

```R
library(DBI)

# Connecting to the database
con <- dbConnect(RSQLite::SQLite(), dbname = "path/to/your/database.sqlite")

# Querying data
data <- dbGetQuery(con, "SELECT * FROM your_table")

# Disconnecting from the database dbDisconnect(con)
```

6.3 Exporting Data

Exporting data is just as important as importing it. R provides several functions and packages to facilitate data export in various formats.

6.3.1 Exporting to CSV Files

To export data to a CSV file, the `write.csv()` function is used. Here's a basic example:

```R
# Exporting data to a CSV file
write.csv(data, "path/to/your/output.csv", row.names = FALSE)
```

```
` ` `
```

`row.names = FALSE` prevents R from adding row numbers as a new column. ### 6.3.2 Exporting to Excel Files

To export data to an Excel file, the `writexl` package can be employed:

```R
library(writexl)
```

Exporting data to an Excel file write_xlsx(data, "path/to/your/output.xlsx")
```
` ` `
```

6.3.3 Exporting to JSON Files

To save your R data frame as a JSON file, you can also use the `jsonlite` package:

```R
library(jsonlite)
```

Exporting data to a JSON file write_json(data, "path/to/your/output.json")
```
` ` `
```

6.3.4 Exporting Data to Databases

Similar to importing, R allows you to export data to databases using the `DBI` package. Here's a simple example of exporting a data frame to a SQLite database:

```R
library(DBI)
```

con <- dbConnect(RSQLite::SQLite(), dbname = "path/to/your/database.sqlite") # Writing data to the database

88

```
dbWriteTable(con, "new_table", data, overwrite = TRUE)
dbDisconnect(con)
```

6.4 Best Practices for Data Importing and Exporting

Data Integrity: Always check for errors or inconsistencies after importing data. Use functions like

`str()` and `summary()` to understand the structure of your data.

Documentation: Document the sources and transformations applied to data. This practice enhances reproducibility and clarity in analysis.

Version Control: Keep track of versions of data files, especially when making substantial changes. It's also helpful to document changes.

Understanding how to efficiently manage data can significantly improve productivity in data analysis workflows. Mastery of these techniques enables researchers and analysts to harness R's full potential for data exploration, visualization, and modeling.

Reading Data from CSV, Excel, and Other Formats

This chapter will guide you through the methods and best practices for reading these data formats into R, enabling you to get started with your data analysis projects.

1. Reading Data from CSV Files

CSV (Comma-Separated Values) is one of the most

common formats for storing tabular data. R provides built-in functions to read CSV files easily.

Using `read.csv()`

The simplest function to read a CSV file in R is `read.csv()`. Here's how you can use it:

```R
# Reading a CSV file into R

data <- read.csv("path/to/your/file.csv")
```

Parameters:

`file`: The path to the CSV file.

`header`: A logical value indicating whether the first row contains column names (`TRUE` by default).

`sep`: The field separator character (comma by default).

`stringsAsFactors`: A logical value to convert strings to factors (`FALSE` by default in recent versions). ### Example

```R
data <- read.csv("my_data.csv", stringsAsFactors = TRUE) head(data) # Preview the first few rows of the dataset
```

Handling Common Issues

Missing Values: R understands certain strings as NA (`NA`, `NULL`, or blank). You can specify additional strings to treat as NA using the `na.strings` parameter.

```R
data <- read.csv("my_data.csv", na.strings = c("", "NA",
"NULL"))
```

2. Reading Excel Files

Excel files are another common format for data storage, and R has several packages to handle them. The

`readxl` package is one of the most popular choices. ### Using `read_excel()`

First, ensure that you have the `readxl` package installed. You can install it using:

```R
install.packages("readxl")
```

Then, you can use the following code to read an Excel file:

```R
library(readxl)
```
Reading an Excel file

```
data <- read_excel("path/to/your/file.xlsx", sheet = 1)
```

Parameters:

`path`: The path to the Excel file.

`sheet`: The name or index of the sheet you want to read. ### Example

```R
library(readxl)
```

```
data <- read_excel("my_data.xlsx", sheet = "Sheet1")
head(data)  # Preview the first few rows of the dataset
```

Notes on Excel Files

The `readxl` package only reads `.xlsx` and `.xls` formats.

If you have multiple sheets, you can specify which one to import using the `sheet` parameter. ## 3. Other Data Formats

Reading Data from JSON Files

JSON (JavaScript Object Notation) is a lightweight data interchange format that is widely used for APIs. The

`jsonlite` package in R allows you to read and write JSON files easily.

```R
install.packages("jsonlite")
```

To read a JSON file:

```R
library(jsonlite)
data <- fromJSON("path/to/your/file.json")
```

Reading Data from XML Files

For XML (eXtensible Markup Language) files, the `XML` package in R is useful.

```R
install.packages("XML")
```

```
```

To read an XML file:

```R
library(XML)

data <- xmlToDataFrame("path/to/your/file.xml")
```

Reading Data from Databases

If your data is stored in a database like MySQL or SQLite, you can use the `DBI` and `RMySQL` or `RSQLite` packages to read data.

```R
install.packages("DBI") install.packages("RSQLite")
```

```R
library(DBI)

con            <-            dbConnect(RSQLite::SQLite(), dbname="my_database.sqlite") data <- dbReadTable(con, "my_table")
```

4. Saving and Exporting Data

After processing your data, you may want to export it back to different formats. You can use `write.csv()` for CSV files and `writexl` for Excel files.

Exporting to CSV

```R
write.csv(data, "output_data.csv", row.names = FALSE)
```

Exporting to Excel

First, install the `writexl` package:

```R
install.packages("writexl")
```

Then use it to export your data:

```R
library(writexl)

write_xlsx(data, "output_data.xlsx")
```

Understanding how to efficiently import and export data formats is crucial for effective data analysis and reporting. As you move forward, practice these techniques with real datasets to build your confidence and proficiency in R programming. With this knowledge, you'll be well-equipped to kick-start your data analysis projects.

Saving and Exporting Data: Keeping Your Work Organized

This chapter delves into the philosophies and practicalities of saving and exporting data in R programming, empowering you with the ability to keep your work structured and accessible.

1. The Importance of Data Management

Before diving into specific methods for saving and exporting data, it's essential to understand why effective data management is important. Data projects can quickly grow in complexity, especially when handling large datasets and numerous outputs. By adopting an organized approach to saving your work, you can:

Enhance Reproducibility: Ensuring that the results of your analysis can be replicated by others (or even by yourself in the future) is paramount. Properly saving your datasets and outputs contributes to reproducibility, an essential principle in data science.

Facilitate Collaboration: When working in teams, clear organization of datasets and results allows team members to easily access and understand each other's contributions.

Enable Efficient Workflow: Knowing where your data is, what format it is in, and how to access it saves time and reduces frustration.

2. Saving R Objects

In R, various functions allow you to save and load R objects efficiently. The two most commonly used functions are `save()` and `saveRDS()`. Understanding the difference between these two methods is vital for effective data management.

2.1 Using `save()`

The `save()` function allows you to save one or more R objects to a specified file in a binary format. This is particularly useful when you want to save the entire workspace or a set of related objects for future use.

Example:

```R
# Sample data
df <- data.frame(A = 1:5, B = letters[1:5])
# Save the dataframe and an additional object
other_object <- list(a = 1, b = 2)
```

```R
save(df, other_object, file = "my_data.RData")
```

To load the saved objects back into your R session, you can use the `load()` function:

```R
load("my_data.RData")
```

2.2 Using `saveRDS()`

The `saveRDS()` function is ideal for saving a single R object to a file in a more efficient way. This function saves the object in a way that you can later load it using `readRDS()` without worrying about naming conflicts.

Example:

```R
# Save a single object
saveRDS(df, file = "my_dataframe.rds")
# Load the object back
loaded_df <- readRDS("my_dataframe.rds")
```

2.3 Choosing Between `save()` and `saveRDS()`

Use `save()` when you need to save multiple objects and want them to be restored in the same names as before.

Use `saveRDS()` when you want to save a single object and retrieve it under a new name. ## 3. Exporting Data to Various Formats

Once your analysis is complete, you may need to share your results or make them accessible to others who might not use R. R provides functions for exporting data in various formats, including CSV, Excel, and databases.

3.1 Exporting to CSV

One of the most widely used formats for data sharing is CSV (Comma-Separated Values). The `write.csv()` function allows you to export data frames to CSV files easily.

Example:

```R

# Exporting the dataframe to a CSV file

write.csv(df, file = "my_dataframe.csv", row.names = FALSE)

```

3.2 Exporting to Excel

For users who prefer Excel spreadsheets, the `writexl` package provides a convenient function
`write_xlsx()`.

Example:

```R

# Install the package (run this line if you haven't installed the package) install.packages("writexl")

library(writexl)

write_xlsx(df, path = "my_dataframe.xlsx")

```

3.3 Connecting to Databases

In data science projects involving databases, you may need to export data directly to database management systems (DBMS). The `DBI` package in R simplifies database connections and operations, allowing you to write data frames directly to a database.

Example:

```R
# Required library install.packages("DBI") library(DBI)

# Establish connection (example with SQLite)

con <- dbConnect(RSQLite::SQLite(), dbname = "my_database.sqlite")

# Writing data frame to a database table dbWriteTable(con, "my_table", df)

# Don't forget to disconnect dbDisconnect(con)
```

4. Organizing Your Files

Beyond simply saving and exporting data, maintaining an organized directory structure is crucial. Here are a few best practices:

Consistent Naming Conventions: Use clear, descriptive names for your files, so others (and future you) can easily understand their contents. A common convention is to include dates or version numbers.

Directory Structure: Organize your project into directories such as `data/`, `scripts/`, `outputs/`, and `figures/`. This makes navigation straightforward and helps delineate different components of your project. Example directory structure:

```
```

```
/my_project/ data/

raw_data.csv cleaned_data.csv

scripts/ data_cleaning.R analysis.R

outputs/ results_summary.csv

figures/ plot1.png
```

```
```

In this chapter, we explored the critical concepts related to saving and exporting data in R programming. By mastering the techniques discussed, you set a strong foundation for organized workflows, which enhances reproducibility and collaboration.

Chapter 7: Data Manipulation with dplyr

Data manipulation is a critical aspect of data analysis, enabling researchers and analysts to transform raw data into meaningful insights. In the R programming language, the `dplyr` package offers a powerful set of tools for data manipulation. This chapter provides an overview of `dplyr`, its key functions, and practical examples to illustrate how to effectively utilize this package. By the end of the chapter, you will have a solid understanding of how to manipulate data frames using `dplyr` and apply these techniques to real-world data.

7.1 What is dplyr?

`dplyr` is a package in R designed specifically for data manipulation. It provides a set of intuitive functions that enable users to filter, select, arrange, and summarize data easily. The syntax of `dplyr` is user-friendly and is built around a set of key verbs that represent common data manipulation tasks. These verbs include:

`filter()`: Used for subsetting rows based on specific conditions.

`select()`: Allows users to choose specific columns in a data frame.

`arrange()`: Sorts the rows of a data frame based on one or more columns.

`mutate()`: Creates new columns or modifies existing ones.

`summarize()`: Reduces data to summary statistics. ## 7.2 Getting Started with dplyr

To begin using `dplyr`, you must first install and load the package. You can install it from CRAN using the following command:

```R
install.packages("dplyr")
```

Once installed, load the package with:

```R
library(dplyr)
```

7.2.1 Data Frame Creation

Before diving into the functions of `dplyr`, let's create a simple data frame for demonstration purposes:

```R
# Creating a sample data frame data <- data.frame(
ID = 1:5,
Name = c("Alice", "Bob", "Charlie", "David", "Eva"), Age = c(23, 34, 45, 29, 31),
Salary = c(70000, 80000, 120000, 90000, 95000)
)
```

7.3 Core Functions of dplyr

Let's now explore the core functions offered by `dplyr`.
7.3.1 Filtering Rows with filter()

The `filter()` function allows you to subset rows based on conditions. For example, if you want to filter employees older than 30, you can use:

```R
# Filtering rows where Age is greater than 30 filtered_data
<- filter(data, Age > 30) print(filtered_data)
```

7.3.2 Selecting Columns with select()

If you need to select specific columns from your data frame, `select()` is the ideal function. For example, to select only the `Name` and `Salary` columns:

```R
# Selecting specific columns

selected_data    <-    select(data,    Name,    Salary)
print(selected_data)
```

7.3.3 Arranging Rows with arrange()

To sort the data by a specific column, you can use the `arrange()` function. For example, to sort the data frame by `Salary` in descending order:

```R
# Arranging rows by Salary in descending order
arranged_data    <-    arrange(data,    desc(Salary))
print(arranged_data)
```

7.3.4 Creating New Columns with mutate()

The `mutate()` function allows you to create new variables or modify existing ones. For example, to add a column for `Salary` after applying a 10% increase:

```R
# Adding a new column for increased salary

data <- mutate(data, Increased_Salary = Salary * 1.10)
print(data)
```

7.3.5 Summarizing Data with summarize()

The `summarize()` function helps you compute summary statistics. For example, if you want to find the average salary of employees:

```R
# Summarizing with average salary

average_salary <- summarize(data, Average_Salary = mean(Salary))

print(average_salary)
```

7.4 Combining dplyr Functions with Pipes

One of the most powerful features of `dplyr` is the ability to combine multiple functions using the pipe operator (`%>%`). This operator allows you to chain functions together, creating a clear and concise workflow. Here's how you can use pipes to filter, select, and summarize data in one fluid command:

```R
# Using pipes to filter, select, and summarize summary <- data %>%

filter(Age > 30) %>% select(Name, Salary) %>%
```

```
summarize(Average_Salary = mean(Salary))
print(summary)
```

7.5 Practical Example

Let's put together what we've learned in a practical scenario. Suppose you have a data frame of employees, and you want to find the average salary of employees above 30 years old, sorted by their names.

```R
# Complete workflow to filter, arrange, and summarize
final_summary <- data %>%

filter(Age > 30) %>% arrange(Name) %>%

summarize(Average_Salary = mean(Salary))

print(final_summary)
```

In this chapter, we explored the fundamentals of data manipulation using the `dplyr` package in R. We covered core functions such as `filter()`, `select()`, `arrange()`, `mutate()`, and `summarize()`. Additionally, we learned how to combine these functions using pipes for an efficient workflow. The capabilities of `dplyr` empower data analysts to transform and analyze data with ease, making it an essential tool in the R programming landscape.

Filtering, Selecting, and Mutating Data

In this chapter, we will delve into various techniques for manipulating data frames, primarily using the `dplyr` package, which is part of the Tidyverse—a collection of R packages designed for data science. ## 5.1 Introduction to dplyr

The `dplyr` package provides a set of functions specifically designed to make data manipulation easier. It introduces a consistent set of verbs, which can be understood as actions that we can take on our data. The most common verbs that we will focus on in this chapter are:

`filter()`: Subsets rows based on specific conditions.

`select()`: Chooses specific columns from a data frame.

`mutate()`: Creates or modifies columns in a data frame. Before we begin, let's ensure that `dplyr` is installed and loaded:

```R
install.packages("dplyr")  # Install dplyr if you haven't already library(dplyr)    # Load dplyr
```

5.2 Filtering Data

The `filter()` function allows you to subset your data frame based on logical conditions. By employing various logical operators, you can select rows that meet specific criteria.

5.2.1 Basic Filtering

Suppose we have a data frame of students with their scores:

```R
```

```R
students <- data.frame(

name = c("Alice", "Bob", "Charlie", "Diana", "Edward"),
score = c(85, 92, 78, 95, 88)

)
```

To filter students with scores greater than 90, we would use:

```R
high_scorers    <-    filter(students,   score   >    90)
print(high_scorers)
```

5.2.2 Combining Conditions

You can also combine multiple filtering conditions using logical operators (`&` for "and", `|` for "or"). For example, to filter students who scored more than 80 and less than 90:

```R
filtered_students <- filter(students, score > 80 & score < 90) print(filtered_students)
```

5.3 Selecting Data

The `select()` function allows you to refine your data frame by choosing specific columns. This can be especially useful when working with large data sets where you only need a subset of the columns.

5.3.1 Selecting Columns

Using our `students` data frame, suppose we want to select only the `name` column:

```R

names_only <- select(students, name) print(names_only)
```

5.3.2 Selecting Multiple Columns

If you want to select multiple columns, simply list them:

```R

score_only <- select(students, name, score) print(score_only)
```

5.3.3 Using Helper Functions

`dplyr` also provides helper functions like `starts_with()`, `ends_with()`, and `contains()` for more complex selections. For example, if we had a wider data frame and wanted to select columns starting with "s", we could do:

```R

# Assuming there are columns like score1, score2, student_id selected_columns <- select(students, starts_with("s"))
```

5.4 Mutating Data

The `mutate()` function enables you to create new columns or modify existing ones based on the existing data. This function is incredibly useful for feature engineering—creating new features from existing data.

5.4.1 Creating a New Column

For example, if we wanted to categorize scores into grades, we could do the following:

```R
students_with_grades <- mutate(students, grade = ifelse(score >= 90, "A",

ifelse(score >= 80, "B", "C")))

print(students_with_grades)
```

5.4.2 Modifying Existing Columns

You can also modify existing columns using the `mutate()` function. For instance, to increase each student's score by 5 points:

```R
students_updated <- mutate(students, score = score + 5)
print(students_updated)
```

5.5 Chaining Operations with %>%

One of the most powerful features of `dplyr` is the ability to chain operations together using the pipe operator (`%>%`). This allows for a more readable and expressive code structure.

5.5.1 Example of Chaining

108

Let's say we want to filter for students with scores above 80, select their names, and then categorize them by grades, all in one line:

```R
result <- students %>% filter(score > 80) %>% select(name, score) %>%

mutate(grade = ifelse(score >= 90, "A",

ifelse(score >= 80, "B", "C")))

print(result)
```

We explored the essential data manipulation functions in R using the `dplyr` package—`filter()`, `select()`, and `mutate()`. We learned how to filter rows, select specific columns, and create or modify columns in a data frame. We also highlighted the convenience of chaining operations with the pipe operator to produce clearer, more concise code.

Grouping and Summarizing Data: Extracting Insights

One of the most effective techniques to derive insights from data is grouping and summarizing it. This chapter focuses on utilizing R programming to manipulate and comprehend datasets through powerful functions and packages, allowing analysts to transform raw data into actionable insights.

Understanding Data Grouping ### What is Grouping?

Grouping involves categorizing data into subsets based on one or more variables. This process retains the structure of the data while facilitating summary statistics and comparisons. For instance, consider a dataset of sales records for multiple stores. If you wish to understand performance differences between stores, grouping the data by the store identifier would be the first step.

Basic Grouping Functions in R

R provides several functions for grouping data, with the most notable being `aggregate()`, `tapply()`, and the `dplyr` package. While base R functions are useful, `dplyr` offers a cleaner and more intuitive syntax for data manipulation tasks.

Using `aggregate()`

The `aggregate()` function allows you to compute summary statistics for each group in your dataset. Here's a basic example:

```r
# Sample data
sales_data <- data.frame(
Store = c("A", "A", "B", "B", "C", "C"), Sales = c(200, 300, 250, 400, 150, 350)
)
# Aggregate sales by Store
agg_sales <- aggregate(Sales ~ Store, data = sales_data, FUN = sum) print(agg_sales)
```

This code will yield the total sales for each store, demonstrating the power of basic grouping in R. ### The Magic of `dplyr`

The `dplyr` package enhances data manipulation, including grouping and summarizing, with functions that promote readability and efficiency. The key functions used in `dplyr` for grouping are `group_by()` and

`summarize()`.

Example with `dplyr`

Here's how you can use `dplyr` to achieve similar results:

```r
r library(dplyr)

# Group and summarize sales agg_sales_dplyr <- sales_data %>% group_by(Store) %>% summarize(Total_Sales = sum(Sales))

print(agg_sales_dplyr)
```

The pipe operator `%>%` enables chaining commands, enhancing readability. The output provides total sales by store similarly to our previous example but with cleaner syntax.

Advanced Summarization Techniques ### Multiple Summaries

When exploring data, one often wants more than just totals. `summarize()` can compute various statistics at once. You can calculate mean, median, and count all in one go:

```r
agg_sales_advanced <- sales_data %>% group_by(Store) %>%

summarize(

Total_Sales = sum(Sales), Average_Sales = mean(Sales),
Sales_Count = n()

)

print(agg_sales_advanced)
```

Using `mutate()` for Additional Calculations

Sometimes, you may want to create new variables based on your grouped data. Using `mutate()` alongside `group_by()` can achieve this seamlessly.

```r
sales_data <- sales_data %>% group_by(Store) %>% mutate(Average_Sales = mean(Sales))

print(sales_data)
```

Visualizing Grouped Data

Visualizations play a key role in data analysis. After summarizing your data, it's essential to convey insights visually. R is equipped with several libraries for this purpose, most notably `ggplot2`.

Creating Visual Representations

Here's an example of how to visualize total sales by store using `ggplot2`:

```r
library(ggplot2)

ggplot(data = agg_sales_dplyr, aes(x = Store, y = Total_Sales)) + geom_bar(stat = "identity", fill = "blue") +

labs(title = "Total Sales by Store", x = "Store", y = "Total Sales")
```

This code produces a bar plot depicting the total sales of each store, making it easier to identify which stores perform best.

We explored the techniques of grouping and summarizing data using R programming. We began with basic functions from base R, progressed to more sophisticated capabilities offered by the `dplyr` package, and concluded by demonstrating how to visualize these insights effectively.

Chapter 8: Data Visualization with ggplot2

In the age of big data, the ability to visualize data effectively can lead to better insights, clearer communication, and more informed decision-making. R programming, with its rich ecosystem of packages, provides various tools for creating detailed and informative visualizations. One of the most popular and versatile among these is `ggplot2`.

What is ggplot2?

`ggplot2` is an R package developed by Hadley Wickham that implements the Grammar of Graphics, a coherent system for describing and building visualizations. It allows practitioners to create a wide range of graphics in a consistent manner by layering components on top of each other.

The key components of `ggplot2` visualization include:

Data: The dataset being visualized.

Aesthetics (aes): The visual properties of the data, such as position, color, shape, and size.

Geometries (geom): The geometric objects that represent the data points, such as points, lines, and bars.

Statistics (stat): Statistical transformations that can be applied to the data, such as summarizing or counting.

Coordinates (coord): The coordinate system used for the plot, which can be adjusted to better present the data.

Facets: A way to split data into subsets to create multiple plots based on categorical variables.

Themes: Customizable elements for improving the overall aesthetics of the plot. ## Getting Started with ggplot2

To utilize `ggplot2`, you first need to ensure that it's installed and loaded into your R environment. You can do this by running the following commands:

```R
install.packages("ggplot2")
library(ggplot2)
```

Let's begin with a simple example using the built-in `mtcars` dataset, which contains information about various car models and their specifications.

Basic Scatter Plot

The scatter plot is one of the fundamental types of visualizations. It can help you visualize the relationship between two numeric variables. Here's how to create a basic scatter plot to visualize the relationship between `mpg` (miles per gallon) and `wt` (weight) of cars:

```R
ggplot(data = mtcars, aes(x = wt, y = mpg)) +
geom_point()
```

This command initializes a ggplot object with the `mtcars` dataset and specifies `wt` as the x-axis and `mpg` as the y-axis. The `geom_point()` function adds points to the plot.

Customizing the Plot

`ggplot2` allows for extensive customization, from changing colors to adding titles. Below is an example that

115

modifies the previous scatter plot by adding a title, changing point color, and altering point size:

```R
ggplot(data = mtcars, aes(x = wt, y = mpg)) + geom_point(color = "blue", size = 3) +

labs(title = "MPG vs Weight of Cars", x = "Weight (1000 lbs)", y = "Miles Per Gallon") + theme_minimal()
```

The `labs()` function is used to add titles and labels, while `theme_minimal()` provides a clean, minimalistic visualization theme.

Adding a Trend Line

To better understand the relationship between `wt` and `mpg`, you might want to add a linear regression line. This can be done using the `geom_smooth()` function:

```R
ggplot(data = mtcars, aes(x = wt, y = mpg)) + geom_point(color = "blue", size = 3) + geom_smooth(method = "lm", se = FALSE, color = "red") +

labs(title = "MPG vs Weight of Cars", x = "Weight (1000 lbs)", y = "Miles Per Gallon") + theme_minimal()
```

Here, `geom_smooth(method = "lm")` adds a linear model fit, and `se = FALSE` omits the confidence interval shading.

Other Types of Plots

`ggplot2` supports a variety of other plot types, including:

Bar Plots: Useful for visualizing categorical data.

```R
ggplot(data = mtcars, aes(x = factor(cyl))) + geom_bar(fill = "steelblue") +
labs(title = "Count of Cars by Cylinder Count", x = "Number of Cylinders", y = "Count") + theme_minimal()
```

Histograms: Ideal for visualizing the distribution of a numeric variable.

```R
ggplot(data = mtcars, aes(x = mpg)) +
geom_histogram(binwidth = 2, fill = "lightblue", color = "black") +
labs(title = "Distribution of Miles Per Gallon", x = "Miles Per Gallon", y = "Count") + theme_minimal()
```

Boxplots: Useful for visualizing the distribution of a numeric variable across different categories.

```R
ggplot(data = mtcars, aes(x = factor(cyl), y = mpg)) +
geom_boxplot(fill = "orange") +
labs(title = "Boxplot of MPG by Cylinder Count", x = "Number of Cylinders", y = "Miles Per Gallon") +
theme_minimal()
```

```
` ` `
```

Faceting with ggplot2

Faceting allows creating multiple plots based on different subsets of the data. This can be particularly helpful for comparing distributions across categories. You can use the `facet_wrap()` function in `ggplot2`. For example:

```R
ggplot(data = mtcars, aes(x = wt, y = mpg)) + geom_point() +

facet_wrap(~ cyl) +

labs(title = "MPG vs Weight Faceted by Cylinder Count", x = "Weight (1000 lbs)", y = "Miles Per Gallon")

+

theme_minimal()
` ` `
```

Here, we create a separate scatter plot for each cylinder count, allowing for easy visual comparisons between groups.

We explored the versatile `ggplot2` package for data visualization in R. From creating basic scatter plots to complex faceted visualizations, the power of `ggplot2` shines through its layered approach to building graphics. Mastering `ggplot2` will provide you with a solid foundation for exploring and presenting your data effectively, making your analyses not just informative but engaging as well.

Creating Basic Plots: Histograms, Scatterplots, and Bar Charts

Visual representation of data is critical in data analysis as it communicates patterns, trends, and insights effectively. In this chapter, we will explore how to create three fundamental types of plots in R: histograms, scatterplots, and bar charts. Each of these visualizations serves distinct purposes and will be discussed with practical examples and code snippets.

1. Histograms ### Overview

Histograms are crucial for displaying the distribution of a continuous variable. They break down the range of data into intervals (or "bins") and count how many data points fall within each bin. This visualization helps in understanding the underlying frequency distribution of the data set.

Creating a Histogram in R

To create a histogram in R, we can use the `hist()` function. Let's start with an example utilizing the built-in dataset, `mtcars`, which contains specifications and performance data for various car models.

```R
```

Load necessary libraries library(ggplot2)

Load the mtcars dataset data(mtcars)

Basic Histogram of the 'mpg' (miles per gallon) variable hist(mtcars$mpg,

main = "Histogram of Miles Per Gallon", xlab = "Miles Per Gallon",

col = "blue", border = "black", breaks = 10)
```

### Explanation of Code

`main` sets the title of the histogram.

`xlab` describes the x-axis.

`col` selects the color of the bars.

`border` specifies the color of the bar borders.

`breaks` defines the number of bins the range of data should be divided into. ### Enhancing Histograms with ggplot2

The `ggplot2` package, a powerful tool for creating sophisticated visualizations, can also be used to create more aesthetically pleasing histograms.

```R
# Using ggplot2 to create a histogram ggplot(mtcars, aes(x = mpg)) + geom_histogram(binwidth = 2,

fill = "blue", color = "black") +

labs(title = "Histogram of Miles Per Gallon", x = "Miles Per Gallon",

y = "Frequency")
```

Key Takeaways

Histograms are instrumental in visualizing the distribution of a dataset. They allow analysts to identify central tendencies, variability, and the presence of outliers
```

visually.

2. Scatterplots ### Overview

Scatterplots are used to depict the relationship between two continuous variables. By plotting one variable along the x-axis and another along the y-axis, scatterplots can reveal correlations, trends, and the degree of relationship between the variables.

Creating a Scatterplot in R

Again using the `mtcars` dataset, let's create a scatterplot to visualize the relationship between horsepower (`hp`) and miles per gallon (`mpg`).

```R
# Basic Scatterplot plot(mtcars$hp,

mtcars$mpg,

main = "Scatterplot of Horsepower vs. MPG", xlab = "Horsepower",

ylab = "Miles Per Gallon", pch = 19,

col = "red")
```

Explanation of Code

`pch` defines the point character used in the plot.

`col` specifies the color of the points. ### Creating Scatterplots with ggplot2

Using `ggplot2` for scatterplots also enhances the appearance and functionality, especially when adding regression lines or other layers.

```R
# Using ggplot2 to create a scatterplot ggplot(mtcars,
aes(x = hp, y = mpg)) + geom_point(color = "red", size =
3) +


labs(title = "Scatterplot of Horsepower vs. MPG", x =
"Horsepower",

y = "Miles Per Gallon") + geom_smooth(method = "lm",
col = "blue")
```

Key Takeaways

Scatterplots provide insights into the relationship between variables, enabling analysts to observe correlations and trends that may not be immediately apparent in raw data.

3. Bar Charts ### Overview

Bar charts are excellent for displaying categorical data. They represent different categories with rectangular bars, where the length of each bar corresponds to the value or count for that category.

Creating a Bar Chart in R

Let's create a simple bar chart to show the counts of cars by the number of cylinders (`cyl`) in the `mtcars` dataset.

```R
# Basic Bar Chart barplot(table(mtcars$cyl),

main = "Number of Cars by Cylinder Count", xlab =
"Number of Cylinders",
```

ylab = "Frequency", col = "lightblue", border = "black")
```

### Explanation of Code

`table()` creates a frequency table of the variable.

Similar to previous plots, `main`, `xlab`, `ylab`, `col`, and `border` serve similar purposes as described earlier.

### Creating Bar Charts with ggplot2

```R
# Using ggplot2 to create a bar chart ggplot(mtcars, aes(x = factor(cyl))) + geom_bar(fill = "lightblue", color = "black") + labs(title = "Number of Cars by Cylinder Count",

x = "Number of Cylinders", y = "Frequency")
```

Key Takeaways

Bar charts are effective for comparing quantities across different categories, making them essential for categorical data analysis.

Visualizing data through histograms, scatterplots, and bar charts is fundamental to data analysis in R programming. Understanding how to create and customize these plots using both base R functions and

`ggplot2` equips analysts with the skills to deliver compelling insights from data. Each type of plot serves a unique purpose, allowing for a deeper understanding of the data's characteristics that purely numerical analysis
```

might overlook.

Customizing Plots: Colors, Themes, and Labels

This chapter will guide you through customizing plots by focusing on colors, themes, and labels, demonstrating how to breathe life into your R visualizations.

Understanding the Basics of Plotting in R

Before diving into customization, let's quickly revisit how to create a basic plot in R. Utilizing the built-in `mtcars` dataset, we'll create a simple scatter plot to establish a foundation.

```R
# Basic Scatter Plot

plot(mtcars$mpg, mtcars$hp, main = "Horsepower vs. Miles per Gallon", xlab = "Miles per Gallon (mpg)", ylab = "Horsepower (hp)")
```

This code generates a scatter plot of horsepower against miles per gallon. While functional, it's rather plain, leading us to explore customization options.

Customizing Colors

Color is fundamental in data visualization, as it can highlight key information and differentiate between datasets. R offers several ways to customize colors.

Basic Color Customization

You can easily change point or line colors using the `col`

argument in plotting functions. R has built-in color names and also allows hexadecimal color codes.

```R
# Scatter Plot with Custom Colors

plot(mtcars$mpg, mtcars$hp, col = "blue", pch = 19, main = "Horsepower vs. Miles per Gallon", xlab = "Miles per Gallon (mpg)", ylab = "Horsepower (hp)")
```

In this example, we change the color of the points to blue and utilize `pch` to modify the point shape. ### Using Color Palettes

To enhance the visual appeal and differentiation in complex plots, consider using color palettes. The

`RColorBrewer` package provides a variety of color palettes that are visually distinctive and suitable for different types of data.

```R
# Installing and loading the RColorBrewer package
install.packages("RColorBrewer") library(RColorBrewer)
```

Scatter Plot with Color Palette

colors <- brewer.pal(n = 3, name = "Set1") plot(mtcars$mpg, mtcars$hp, col = colors[1], pch = 19)

points(mtcars$mpg[mtcars$cyl == 4], mtcars$hp[mtcars$cyl == 4], col = colors[2], pch = 19)

points(mtcars$mpg[mtcars$cyl == 8], mtcars$hp[mtcars$cyl == 8], col = colors[3], pch = 19)

```
```

Advanced Color Customization

For more complex visualizations, consider using the `ggplot2` package, which offers more options for color customization.

```R
```

Using ggplot2 for Custom Colors library(ggplot2)

ggplot(mtcars, aes(x = mpg, y = hp, color = factor(cyl))) + geom_point(size = 3) +

scale_color_manual(values = c("red", "green", "blue")) +

labs(title = "Horsepower vs. Miles per Gallon", x = "Miles per Gallon (mpg)", y = "Horsepower (hp)", color

= "Cylinders")

```
```

Here, we differentiate points by cylinder count using distinct colors. ## Customizing Themes

Themes in R, particularly when using `ggplot2`, allow you to apply a cohesive set of appearance settings to your entire plot. Themes control background colors, grid lines, and more.

Built-in Themes

`ggplot2` comes with several built-in themes. You can easily switch between them to find one that suits your visualization style.

```R
```

Applying Themes in ggplot2 ggplot(mtcars, aes(x = mpg,

```
y = hp)) + geom_point() +
theme_minimal() +
labs(title = "Horsepower vs. Miles per Gallon", x = "Miles
per Gallon (mpg)", y = "Horsepower (hp)")
```

Custom Themes

You can create your own themes by customizing various elements to meet your specific needs.

```R
# Custom Theme Example my_theme <- theme(
plot.title  =  element_text(size  =  16,  face  =  "bold"),
axis.title.x = element_text(size = 14),

axis.title.y = element_text(size = 14), panel.background =
element_rect(fill = "lightgray")
)
ggplot(mtcars, aes(x = mpg, y = hp)) + geom_point() +


my_theme +
labs(title = "Horsepower vs. Miles per Gallon", x = "Miles
per Gallon (mpg)", y = "Horsepower (hp)")
```

Customizing Labels

Labels are essential for explaining the data being presented. Customizing titles, axis labels, and legends enhances comprehension.

Adding Titles and Labels

You can add titles and labels for axes using the `main`, `xlab`, and `ylab` parameters in standard R plotting functions. In `ggplot2`, use the `labs()` function.

```R
# Customizing Labels in Base R

plot(mtcars$mpg, mtcars$hp, main = "Customized Horsepower vs. MPG", xlab = "Miles per Gallon", ylab = "Horsepower")
```

```R
# Customizing Labels in ggplot2 ggplot(mtcars, aes(x = mpg, y = hp)) + geom_point() +

labs(title = "Customized Horsepower vs. MPG", x = "Miles per Gallon", y = "Horsepower")
```

Modifying Legend Titles

In `ggplot2`, you can modify legend titles directly through the `labs()` function.

```R
ggplot(mtcars, aes(x = mpg, y = hp, color = factor(cyl))) + geom_point(size = 3) +

labs(title = "Horsepower vs. MPG by Cylinder Count", x = "Miles per Gallon (mpg)", y = "Horsepower (hp)", color = "Number of Cylinders")
```

128

Customization is key to creating effective visualizations in R. By leveraging colors, themes, and labels, you can enhance the communication of your data. Throughout this chapter, we explored various approaches to customizing your plots, from basic color changes to advanced theming options in `ggplot2`.

Chapter 9: Statistical Analysis in R

In this chapter, we will explore the key features of R that facilitate statistical analysis, learn how to implement various statistical methods, and understand how to interpret the results effectively.

9.1 Introduction to R

R is an open-source programming language and software environment for statistical computing and graphics. Its versatility, efficiency, and extensive range of packages make it a favorite among statisticians, data scientists, and researchers. R provides a rich ecosystem, including built-in functions for a wide array of statistical analyses, data manipulation, and powerful visualization tools that help in interpreting data.

9.1.1 Installation and Setup

To start using R for your statistical analysis, you need to download and install R from [CRAN](https://cran.r-project.org/). Many users also opt for RStudio, an integrated development environment (IDE) that makes working with R easier. RStudio provides a user-friendly interface, syntax highlighting, and various tools for package management and project organization.

9.1.2 Basic R Syntax

Once you have R set up, familiarize yourself with some basic syntax. R operates primarily through vectors, data frames, arrays, and lists. Here are some fundamental commands to get you started:

```r
# Create a vector numbers <- c(1, 2, 3, 4, 5)
```

```
# Create a data frame
data <- data.frame(Name = c("Alice", "Bob", "Charlie"),
Age = c(25, 30, 35))
# View the data frame print(data)
```

9.2 Descriptive Statistics

Descriptive statistics summarize and describe the characteristics of a dataset. R offers numerous functions to calculate measures such as mean, median, mode, variance, and standard deviation.

9.2.1 Calculating Descriptive Statistics

Here, we demonstrate how to calculate descriptive statistics using R:

```r
# Load necessary libraries library(dplyr)
# Sample data
data <- c(10, 12, 10, 15, 18, 20)


# Mean
mean_value <- mean(data)
# Median
median_value <- median(data)
# Standard Deviation std_dev <- sd(data)
# Summary
summary_stats <- summary(data)
```

```
# Display results
cat("Mean:", mean_value, "\n") cat("Median:", median_value, "\n") cat("Standard Deviation:", std_dev, "\n") print(summary_stats)
```

9.3 Inferential Statistics

Inferential statistics allow us to infer properties of a population based on sample data. This section will cover hypothesis testing, confidence intervals, and regression analysis.

9.3.1 Hypothesis Testing

Hypothesis testing is fundamental in statistical analysis. In R, functions like `t.test()` allow us to perform t-tests to compare means. Below is an example of a one-sample t-test.

```r
# One-sample t-test
t_test_result <- t.test(data, mu = 15) print(t_test_result)
```

9.3.2 Confidence Intervals

Confidence intervals provide a range of values that likely contain the population parameter. Here's how to calculate a confidence interval in R:

```r
# Confidence Interval
conf_interval <- t.test(data)$conf.int
```

```r
cat("95% Confidence Interval:", conf_interval, "\n")
```

9.3.3 Linear Regression

Linear regression is used to model the relationship between a dependent variable and one or more independent variables. R makes it easy to perform linear regression analysis.

```r
# Sample dataset
df <- data.frame(x = c(1, 2, 3, 4, 5), y = c(2, 3, 5, 7, 11))


# Linear model
model <- lm(y ~ x, data = df) summary(model)
# Plotting the data and regression line
plot(df$x, df$y, main = "Linear Regression", xlab = "X values", ylab = "Y values") abline(model, col = "red")
```

9.4 Advanced Statistical Techniques

Beyond basic analyses, R provides functionality for more advanced statistical techniques, such as ANOVA, chi-squared tests, and time series analysis.

9.4.1 ANOVA

Analysis of Variance (ANOVA) is used to compare the means of three or more groups. Use the `aov()` function to perform ANOVA in R.

```r
```

```
# Sample data
group1 <- c(20, 21, 22)
group2 <- c(30, 31, 29)
group3 <- c(25, 24, 26)
# Combine data into a data frame
data_anova <- data.frame(values = c(group1, group2, group3),
group = factor(rep(c("Group1", "Group2", "Group3"), each = 3)))
# ANOVA test
anova_result <- aov(values ~ group, data = data_anova)
summary(anova_result)
```

9.4.2 Chi-Squared Test

The chi-squared test is used to determine if there is a significant association between categorical variables.

```r
# Sample data
observed <- matrix(c(30, 10, 20, 40), nrow = 2) chisq_test <- chisq.test(observed) print(chisq_test)
```

9.5 Visualization

Visualization is a critical component of statistical analysis, as it helps communicate findings effectively. R provides several libraries for creating informative visualizations, including `ggplot2`, which is renowned for its flexibility and elegance.

9.5.1 Creating Plots with ggplot2

Here's how to create a basic scatter plot and histogram using `ggplot2`.

```r
# Load the ggplot2 library library(ggplot2)
# Scatter plot
ggplot(df, aes(x = x, y = y)) + geom_point() +
geom_smooth(method = "lm", col = "red") +
ggtitle("Scatter Plot with Linear Regression Line")
# Histogram
ggplot(data.frame(data), aes(x = data)) +
geom_histogram(binwidth = 1, fill = "blue", color =
"white") + ggtitle("Histogram of Data")
```

We explored the fundamental aspects of statistical analysis using R, including descriptive statistics, inferential statistics, and advanced statistical techniques. R's comprehensive functionality, combined with its visualization capabilities, makes it a powerful tool for data analysis. As you continue to work with R, the skills and insights gained here will serve as a solid foundation for conducting statisticaz analyses on real-world datasets.

Descriptive Statistics: Mean, Median, Variance, and More

This chapter will delve into several key concepts of descriptive statistics including mean, median, variance, standard deviation, range, and interquartile range (IQR), all while utilizing R, a powerful programming language often used for statistical computing and data visualization. We will explore how to calculate these statistics using built-in R functions and through practical examples.

Understanding Descriptive Statistics

Descriptive statistics aim to describe the general characteristics of a dataset. While they do not allow for conclusions beyond the immediate data, they offer vital insights into patterns, correlations, and anomalies within the data. Below are some of the most commonly used descriptive statistics:

Mean: The average of the data points.

Median: The middle value when the data points are ordered.

Variance: A measure of the data's spread around the mean.

Standard Deviation: The square root of variance, indicating the average distance of each data point from the mean.

Range: The difference between the maximum and minimum values in the dataset.

Interquartile Range (IQR): The range of the middle 50% of the data points, calculated as the difference between the first (Q1) and third (Q3) quartiles.

Getting Started with R

Before we dive into descriptive statistics, it's important to have R installed on your system. You can download R from the [CRAN website](https://cran.r-project.org/). Additionally, using RStudio, an integrated development environment for R, can enhance your programming experience.

Once R is set up, you can start by loading or creating a dataset. For demonstration purposes, let's create a simple dataset:

```R
# Create a dataset of exam scores

scores <- c(78, 85, 95, 88, 72, 90, 94, 83, 87, 91)
```

Calculating Mean and Median

The mean and median are two primary measures of central tendency. Here's how to compute them in R:

```R
# Calculate the mean mean_score <- mean(scores)
print(paste("Mean Score:", mean_score))
# Calculate the median median_score <- median(scores)
print(paste("Median Score:", median_score))
```

Interpretation:

The **mean** might be heavily influenced by outliers,

while the **median** provides a robust central value, especially in skewed distributions.

Exploring Variance and Standard Deviation

Variance and standard deviation are key to understanding the spread of the dataset. Here's how to compute them:

```R
# Calculate variance variance_score <- var(scores)

print(paste("Variance:", variance_score))

# Calculate standard deviation sd_score <- sd(scores)

print(paste("Standard Deviation:", sd_score))
```

Interpretation:

A low variance indicates that the data points tend to be close to the mean. Conversely, a high variance shows that the data points are spread out over a wider range.

Understanding Range and Interquartile Range (IQR)

The range gives a sense of the extremes of the data, while the IQR focuses on the central 50%. Here's how to calculate both:

```R
# Calculate range range_score <- range(scores)

print(paste("Range:    From",    range_score[1],    "to", range_score[2]))

# Calculate IQR iqr_score <- IQR(scores)

print(paste("Interquartile Range (IQR):", iqr_score))
```

```
```

Interpretation:

The **range** gives a quick overview of dispersion, while the **IQR** helps to understand the spread of the middle half of the data, minimizing the impact of outliers.

Visualizing Descriptive Statistics

In addition to calculations, visualizations can be a powerful tool for understanding the data distribution. Using R, you can create boxplots and histograms:

```R
# Boxplot

boxplot(scores, main="Boxplot of Exam Scores", ylab="Scores")

# Histogram

hist(scores, main="Histogram of Exam Scores", xlab="Scores", col="blue", breaks=10)
```

Interpretation of Visualizations:

A **boxplot** provides a visual summary of the median, quartiles, and potential outliers, while a

histogram illustrates the frequency distribution of the data.

In this chapter, we explored the fundamental concepts of descriptive statistics, including mean, median, variance, standard deviation, range, and interquartile range, using R programming. We also visualized our findings to better understand the data.

This foundational knowledge serves as a stepping stone towards more complex statistical analyses and interpretations, empowering you to make data-driven decisions with confidence. In the next chapter, we will delve deeper into inferential statistics and hypothesis testing methods in R.

Inferential Statistics: Hypothesis Testing and Confidence Intervals

While descriptive statistics summarize data through measures such as mean, median, and mode, inferential statistics allows us to make predictions and generalizations about a population based on a sample. Two key concepts in inferential statistics are hypothesis testing and confidence intervals, both of which can be efficiently conducted using the R programming language.

Hypothesis Testing

Hypothesis testing is a statistical method used to determine whether there is enough evidence to reject a null hypothesis. The null hypothesis (Ho) represents a statement of no effect or no difference, while the alternative hypothesis (H1) represents what we aim to prove.

Steps in Hypothesis Testing

Formulate Hypotheses: Clearly define the null and alternative hypotheses. For example:

Ho: = 0 (The population mean is equal to a specified value)

140

H1: 0 (The population mean is not equal to the specified value)

Select a Significance Level (): Commonly set at 0.05, the significance level is the probability of rejecting the null hypothesis when it is true.

Choose the Appropriate Test: Depending on the data type and distribution, select a suitable statistical test (e.g., t-test, chi-squared test, ANOVA).

Calculate the Test Statistic: Using the selected test to compute the test statistic based on the sample data.

Determine p-value or Critical Value: Compare the test statistic to critical values or compute the p- value to make a decision.

Make a Decision: If the p-value is less than or the test statistic exceeds the critical value, reject Ho; otherwise, do not reject Ho.

Example: One-Sample t-Test in R

```R
# Sample data
data <- c(22, 24, 19, 25, 30, 26, 21)
# Hypothesized population mean mu0 <- 23
# Perform one-sample t-test t_test_result <- t.test(data, mu = mu0)
# Display results print(t_test_result)
```

In this example, we have a sample of data and we are testing whether its mean is different from 23. The

`t.test()` function in R computes the t-statistic, degrees of freedom, p-value, and confidence interval for the mean.

Confidence Intervals

A confidence interval provides a range of values that likely contain the true population parameter. It gives us an idea of the uncertainty associated with sample estimates. The most common confidence level is 95%, which means we can be 95% confident that the interval contains the true mean value.

Constructing Confidence Intervals

Calculate Sample Statistics: Determine the sample mean and standard deviation.

Determine the Standard Error (SE): The standard error of the mean (SEM) is calculated as:

$$
SEM = \frac{s}{\sqrt{n}}
$$

where s is the sample standard deviation and n is the sample size.

Choose the Confidence Level: Decide on the desired confidence level (e.g., 95%).

Find the Critical Value: Using the t-distribution, find the critical t-value for the chosen confidence level.

Calculate the Confidence Interval: The confidence interval can be constructed as:

$$
CI = \bar{x} \pm (t_{critical} \times SEM)
$$

where $\bar{x}$ is the sample mean.

Example: Confidence Interval for the Mean in R

```R
# Sample data
data <- c(22, 24, 19, 25, 30, 26, 21)
# Calculate the confidence interval ci_result <- t.test(data)
# Display confidence interval print(ci_result$conf.int)
```

In this example, we leverage the `t.test()` function, which not only performs the hypothesis test but also calculates the confidence interval simultaneously.

Understanding the differences between these concepts and their correct applications is essential for drawing valid conclusions from data. As data analysis continues to expand across various fields, mastering these inferential statistics techniques will empower individuals to make informed decisions based on statistical evidence.

Chapter 10: Handling and Cleaning Data

Cleaning and handling data in R is an essential skill for any data analyst or data scientist. This chapter will guide you through the fundamental techniques for handling and cleaning data in R, ensuring you are well- equipped to prepare your datasets for analysis.

10.1 Understanding the Importance of Data Cleaning

Before diving into the methods, it's critical to understand why data cleaning is vital. Poor quality data can lead to incorrect analyses, misleading visualizations, and unfounded conclusions. Data quality can be impacted by missing values, duplicated records, inconsistencies in data formats, and outliers. By taking the time to clean your data, you improve the reliability and validity of your results.

Common Data Issues:

Missing Values: Incomplete data can result from various factors, including data entry errors or nonresponses in surveys.

Duplicates: Duplicate records in datasets can bias your results and should be identified and removed.

Inconsistent Data: Data entered in different formats can cause issues (e.g., "NY" vs. "New York").

Outliers: Extreme values may indicate errors or unique insights, requiring careful consideration before removal or further analysis.

10.2 Loading Data into R

Before cleaning your data, you need to import it into R. R provides various functions to load data from different formats, including CSV, Excel, and databases.

Example: Loading Data from a CSV File

```R
# Load the necessary libraries library(readr)
```

```R
# Read the CSV file into a dataframe

data <- read_csv("path/to/your/datafile.csv")
```

10.3 Exploring Data

Once your data is loaded, the next step is to understand its structure and contents. R provides various functions for exploring data:

`str()`: Displays the structure of the data frame.

`summary()`: Provides a summary of each variable in the data frame.

`head()`: Shows the first few rows of the data, allowing you to quickly inspect the contents.

Example:

```R
# Display the structure of the data str(data)
```

```R
# Show a summary of the data summary(data)
```

```R
# View the first few rows head(data)
```

10.4 Identifying and Handling Missing Values

Missing values can be handled in various ways, including deletion, imputation, or employing algorithms that accommodate missing data. R has built-in functions for identifying and dealing with missing values.

Identifying Missing Values

```R
# Count the number of missing values in each column
colSums(is.na(data))
```

Handling Missing Values

Removing Rows with Missing Values:

```R
clean_data <- na.omit(data)
```

Imputation: Filling in missing values can be done using the `mice` package:

```R
library(mice)

imputed_data <- mice(data, m=5, method='pmm', maxit=50)
completed_data <- complete(imputed_data)
```

10.5 Removing Duplicates

Duplicate records can skew your analysis, so detecting and removing duplicates is crucial. ### Example of Removing Duplicates

```R
# Remove duplicate rows
clean_data <- data[!duplicated(data), ]
```

10.6 Standardizing Data

Data may come in different formats or conventions. Standardization is an essential step in cleaning data. ### Example: Standardizing Variable Names

To make your column names more manageable, you can use the `janitor` package:

```R library(janitor)
# Clean column names by removing spaces and special characters data <- clean_names(data)
```

Example: Standardizing Text Data

Standardizing values in categorical variables (e.g., transforming "NY" to "New York").

```R
data$state <- recode(data$state, "NY" = "New York", "CA" = "California")
```

10.7 Handling Outliers

Outliers can skew your analysis. They can be identified using various methods, such as boxplots or the Z- score method.

Identifying Outliers with Boxplots
147

```R boxplot(data$variable)
```

Removing Outliers

You can remove outliers based on a defined threshold (e.g., values beyond 1.5 * IQR).

```R

Q1    <-    quantile(data$variable,    0.25)    Q3    <-
quantile(data$variable, 0.75)

IQR <- Q3 - Q1

data  <-  data[data$variable  >=  (Q1  -  1.5  *  IQR)  &
data$variable <= (Q3 + 1.5 * IQR), ]
```

10.8 Reshaping and Aggregating Data

Once your data is clean, you may need to reshape or aggregate it for analysis. The `tidyverse` framework, particularly the `dplyr` and `tidyr` packages, makes these tasks efficient.

Example: Reshaping Data

```R library(dplyr) library(tidyr)

# Pivoting longer or wider data_long <- data %>%

pivot_longer(cols  =  starts_with("var"),  names_to  =
"variable", values_to = "value")

# Grouping and summarizing data summary_data <- data
%>% group_by(categorical_variable) %>%

summarize(mean_value = mean(numeric_variable, na.rm
= TRUE))

148
```

```
```

In this chapter, we covered the significance of handling and cleaning data in R, along with practical methods for identifying and rectifying common data quality issues, including missing values, duplicates, and inconsistencies. Mastering these cleaning techniques is paramount for accurate analyses and insights. By ensuring that your data is clean and well-structured, you pave the way for effective visualizations and robust conclusions.

Detecting and Handling Missing Values

This chapter aims to guide you through the process of detecting and handling missing values in R, ensuring that your analysis remains robust and reliable.

Understanding Missing Values

Missing values are a common occurrence in datasets, often due to various reasons such as data collection errors, non-responses in surveys, or equipment malfunctions. In R, missing values are represented by `NA` (Not Available). Recognizing and addressing these values is a critical step in the data cleaning process.

Types of Missing Data

Missing Completely at Random (MCAR): The likelihood of an observation being missing is completely independent of any observed or unobserved data. The analysis remains unbiased, and methods like listwise deletion can be applied without concern.

Missing at Random (MAR): The missingness is

related to some of the observed data but not the missing values themselves. Imputation techniques can often help recover the lost information effectively.

Missing Not at Random (MNAR): The missingness relates directly to the unobserved data itself. This situation requires more complex modeling approaches or sensitivity analyses.

Detecting Missing Values in R

Before handling missing values, it is paramount to identify their presence in your dataset. Here are some essential functions in R for detecting missing values:

1. `is.na()`

The `is.na()` function checks for `NA` values in a vector, data frame, or matrix.

```R
# Example: Checking for NAs in a vector data_vector <-
c(1, 2, NA, 4, NA, 6) is.na(data_vector)
```

2. `sum(is.na())`

This combination provides the total count of `NA` values in the dataset.

```R
# Example: Total number of missing values in a data
frame data_frame <- data.frame(a = c(1, 2, NA), b = c(4,
NA, 6)) sum(is.na(data_frame))
```

3. `na.omit()`

This function allows you to remove rows with any missing values.

```R
# Example: Removing rows with NAs clean_data <-
na.omit(data_frame)
```

4. `colSums(is.na())`

To get the count of missing values for each column, `colSums(is.na())` is useful.

```R
# Example: Counting NAs in each column of a data frame
na_count <- colSums(is.na(data_frame))
```

5. `anyNA()`

This function checks if there are any missing values in the dataset.

```R
# Example: Check if there are any NAs
anyNA(data_frame)
```

Handling Missing Values

Once you have identified the missing values in your dataset, the next step is to determine how to handle them. Here are various strategies that can be employed in R:

1. Remove Missing Values

Removing rows or columns with missing values is the simplest approach, but it can lead to loss of valuable data.

```R
# Example: Removing rows with any missing values
cleaned_data <- na.omit(data_frame)
```

2. Imputation

Imputation involves replacing missing values with substituted values. Common methods include mean, median, or mode imputation. The `tidyverse` package provides beneficial functions to help with imputation.

Mean Imputation

```R
# Example: Mean imputation for a specific column
data_frame$a[is.na(data_frame$a)]            <- mean(data_frame$a, na.rm = TRUE)
```

Median Imputation

```R
# Example: Median imputation for a specific column
data_frame$b[is.na(data_frame$b)]            <- median(data_frame$b, na.rm = TRUE)
```

Mode Imputation

R does not have a built-in mode function, but you can

create one:

```R
# Function to calculate mode get_mode <- function(v) {
uniq_v <- unique(v)

uniq_v[which.max(tabulate(match(v, uniq_v)))]

}

#          Example:          Mode          imputation
data_frame$b[is.na(data_frame$b)]                    <-
get_mode(data_frame$b)
```

3. Predictive Imputation

You can use algorithms (e.g., linear regression, k-Nearest Neighbors) to predict the missing values based on available data. Packages like `mice` (Multivariate Imputation via Chained Equations) are handy.

```R
# Example: Using the mice package library(mice)

imputed_data <- mice(data_frame, m = 5, method = 'pmm') # predictive mean matching completed_data <- complete(imputed_data)
```

4. Using R's `tidyverse`

The `tidyverse` framework includes tools such as `dplyr` and `tidyr` that simplify the handling of missing values.

- **Filling missing values**:

```R library(dplyr)
```

```R
data_frame <- data_frame %>%
mutate(b = ifelse(is.na(b), mean(b, na.rm = TRUE), b))
```

- **Dropping columns**:

```R
data_frame <- data_frame %>%
select(where(~sum(is.na(.)) < nrow(.)))  # Keep columns with less than 100% NAs
```

Handling missing values appropriately is crucial for maintaining the quality of your data analysis. R provides a comprehensive suite of tools to identify and manage these missing values effectively. Understanding the nature of the missing data, employing suitable methods for detection, and making informed choices about imputation will help you maintain the integrity of your analysis.

Data Transformation Techniques for Better Analysis

This chapter explores various data transformation techniques in R, highlighting their importance and practical application to enhance data analysis.

Understanding Data Transformation

Data transformation refers to the process of converting data from one format or structure into another. This process is essential for cleaning, preparing, and optimizing data for analysis. Effective data transformation can lead to improved accuracy in statistical modeling, more meaningful visualizations, and better insights.

Common Data Transformation Techniques ### 1. Data Cleaning

Before analysis, it is vital to clean the data. This includes handling missing values, removing duplicates, and correcting errors. In R, functions like `na.omit()`, `complete.cases()`, and `duplicated()` can be used.

Example: Handling Missing Values

```R
# Load necessary library library(dplyr)

# Example data frame

data <- data.frame(Name = c("Alice", "Bob", NA, "David"), Score = c(85, NA, 90, 80))

# Remove rows with any missing values cleaned_data <- na.omit(data)
```

2. Data Scaling

Scaling is an essential technique to bring different features of the data onto a similar scale. This is crucial for algorithms sensitive to the scale of data, such as k-means clustering and k-nearest neighbors.

Example: Normalizing Data

```R
# Scale the Score column to have a mean of 0 and standard deviation of 1 scaled_data <- scale(data$Score, center = TRUE, scale = TRUE)
```

```
```

3. Data Aggregation

Aggregation allows the summarization of data into more manageable formats. This can involve computing averages, sums, or counts based on certain categories.

Example: Aggregating Data

```R
```

```
# Aggregate scores by names aggregated_data <- data %>% group_by(Name) %>%

summarise(Mean_Score = mean(Score, na.rm = TRUE))
```

```
```

4. Reshaping Data

Reshaping data is essential for changing the structure of a dataset. In R, you can use functions such as

`pivot_longer()` and `pivot_wider()` from the `tidyr` package to transform data between long and wide formats.

Example: Reshaping Data

```R
```

```
# Load tidyr package library(tidyr)
```

```
# Wide format data wide_data <- data.frame(
```

```
Name = c("Alice", "Bob", "David"), Math = c(85, 90, 75),
```

```
Science = c(80, 85, 70)
```

```
)
```

```
# Convert to long format
```

```
long_data <- pivot_longer(wide_data, cols = c(Math,
Science), names_to = "Subject", values_to = "Score")
```

5. Feature Engineering

Feature engineering involves creating new variables from existing ones, which can provide more predictive power in modeling. This can include transformations, combinations, or binning techniques.

Example: Creating a New Feature

```R
# Create a new feature for Pass/Fail based on score data <- data %>%

mutate(Status = if_else(Score >= 75, "Pass", "Fail"))
```

6. Log Transformation

Log transformation is often used to make skewed distributions more normal. This can improve the performance of many statistical models.

Example: Applying Log Transformation

```R
# Apply log transformation to the Score

data$Log_Score <- log(data$Score + 1) # Adding 1 to handle zeros
```

Visualization of Transformed Data

After transforming the data, visualizations play a crucial role in understanding the results. R offers a suite of visualization packages like `ggplot2` which can help you visualize transformed data effectively.

Example: Visualizing with ggplot2

```R
library(ggplot2)

# Create a bar plot of mean scores by status ggplot(data, aes(x = Status, y = Score)) + geom_bar(stat = "identity") +

labs(title = "Mean Scores by Status", x = "Status", y = "Mean Score")
```

Mastering data transformation techniques in R is essential for anyone looking to conduct thorough data analysis. Through effective cleaning, scaling, aggregation, reshaping, feature engineering, and transformation, analysts can derive more insightful conclusions from their datasets.

Chapter 11: Working with Dates and Times in R

Whether you're analyzing time series data, scheduling events, or simply trying to log timestamps, understanding how to work with dates and times in R is crucial. This chapter will provide an overview of R's capabilities for handling dates and times, including classes, functions, and best practices.

11.1 Understanding Date and Time Classes

R provides several classes to handle date and time data efficiently:

11.1.1 Date Class

The `Date` class in R represents dates in the format "YYYY-MM-DD". It allows for standard operations such as addition, subtraction, and comparison.

```r
# Creating Date objects

date1 <- as.Date("2023-10-30") date2 <- as.Date("2023-11-01")

# Displaying dates print(date1) print(date2)

# Date arithmetic date_diff <- date2 - date1

print(date_diff) # Difference in days
```

11.1.2 POSIXct and POSIXlt Classes

For more complex time-related tasks, R provides the `POSIXct` and `POSIXlt` classes that represent date-times.

- **POSIXct**: This class represents date-time as the number of seconds since the Epoch (1970-01-01).

```r
# Creating POSIXct objects
datetime1 <- as.POSIXct("2023-10-30 12:34:56")
print(datetime1)
```

- **POSIXlt**: This class stores date-time as a list of separate components (seconds, minutes, hours, days, etc.).

```r
# Creating POSIXlt objects
datetime2 <- as.POSIXlt("2023-10-30 12:34:56")
print(datetime2)
```

11.1.3 The `lubridate` Package

For simpler manipulation and parsing of dates and times, the `lubridate` package is highly recommended. It offers functions like `ymd()`, `mdy()`, and `dmy()` for intuitive date creation.

```r
library(lubridate)
# Creating a date using lubridate date3 <- ymd("2023-10-30")
print(date3)
```

```r
# Parsing date-time strings
datetime3 <- ymd_hms("2023-10-30 12:34:56")
print(datetime3)
```

11.2 Formatting Dates and Times

Formatting dates and times for output can be accomplished using the `format()` function in base R or the
`strftime()` function.

```r
# Formatting Date
formatted_date <- format(date3, "%B %d, %Y")
print(formatted_date) # Output: "October 30, 2023"

# Formatting POSIXct
formatted_datetime <- format(datetime1, "%Y-%m-%d %H:%M:%S") print(formatted_datetime) # Output: "2023-10-30 12:34:56"
```

11.3 Extracting and Modifying Components of Dates and Times

You can easily extract or modify parts of dates and times using built-in functions. ### 11.3.1 Extracting Components

You can use the `as.POSIXlt()` function to get components of date-time objects.

```r
```

```r
# Extracting components
lt <- as.POSIXlt(datetime1)
# Accessing parts  year <- lt$year + 1900 month <- lt$mon + 1 day <- lt$mday
print(paste(year, month, day, sep = "-"))
```

11.3.2 Modifying Dates and Times

You can update the components directly by manipulating the objects.

```r
# Adding days date4 <- date3 + 5 print(date4)
# Changing a specific component lt$hour <- 8
new_time <- as.POSIXct(lt) print(new_time)
```

11.4 Handling Time Zones

R can also manage time zones, which is essential for datasets that span multiple regions.

```r
# Setting time zone attr(datetime1, "tzone") <- "UTC"
attr(datetime2, "tzone") <- "America/New_York"
# Converting time zones
datetime_ny <- with_tz(datetime1, "America/New_York") print(datetime_ny)
```

```
```

11.5 Time Series Analysis

R is powerful for time series analysis, with functions and packages designed for this purpose. The `ts` class and the `xts` and `zoo` packages enable sophisticated date-time indexing and time series operation.

```r
# Time series creation

ts_data <- ts(c(1, 3, 2, 5, 6), start = c(2023, 10), frequency = 12) print(ts_data)
```

11.6 Practical Examples

To solidify your understanding, let's take a look at a few practical examples of working with dates and times in R.

11.6.1 Example: Analyzing Daily Sales Data

```r
# Creating a data frame with sales data sales_data <- data.frame(

date = seq(as.Date("2023-10-01"), as.Date("2023-10-10"), by = "day"), sales = c(100, 150, 200, 90, 300, 250, 180, 220, 240, 320)

)

# Analyzing sales

daily_average          <-          mean(sales_data$sales) print(daily_average)
```

11.6.2 Example: Time Series Forecasting

```r
library(forecast)
# Creating a time series
sales_ts <- ts(sales_data$sales, start = c(2023, 10), frequency = 1)
# Forecasting future sales
forecasted_sales <- forecast(sales_ts, h = 3)
print(forecasted_sales)
```

This chapter covered the essential components of R's date-time capabilities, including the use of the

`lubridate` package for simplified parsing and manipulation. Whether you are conducting time series analysis or performing date arithmetic, R provides the tools necessary to effectively manage date-time data in your analyses.

Date and Time Formatting: Lubridate Package Basics

The `lubridate` package in R simplifies many common date-time tasks, making it an essential tool in your data wrangling toolkit. This chapter explores the fundamental functions and features of the `lubridate` package, providing a foundation for managing date and time data effectively.

1. Getting Started with Lubridate ### 1.1 Installation

To begin using the `lubridate` package, you first need to

install it if you haven't already. You can do this from the R console:

```R install.packages("lubridate")
```

After installation, load the package:

```R library(lubridate)
```

1.2 Basic Usage

The `lubridate` package allows you to parse dates and times from various formats into R date-time objects effortlessly. Its intuitive functions and consistent naming conventions are designed to be user-friendly, reducing the learning curve associated with date-time manipulations.

2. Parsing Dates and Times

Lubridate provides several functions to parse date and time data from strings into R date-time objects. Here are the primary functions:

2.1 ymd(), dmy(), mdy()

These functions are among the most commonly used in `lubridate`. They convert character vectors containing date information into Date objects.

`ymd()`: Parses dates in "year-month-day" format.

`dmy()`: Parses dates in "day-month-year" format.

`mdy()`: Parses dates in "month-day-year" format.

```R
# Example of parsing dates date_1 <- ymd("2023-10-12")
```

```
date_2 <- dmy("12-10-2023") date_3 <- mdy("10-12-2023")

print(date_1) # [1] "2023-10-12"
print(date_2) # [1] "2023-10-12"
print(date_3) # [1] "2023-10-12"
```
```

### 2.2 ymd_hms(), dmy_hms(), mdy_hms()

For date-time parsing, `lubridate` extends these functions with time components:

**`ymd_hms()`**:          For          "year-month-day hour:minute:second".

**`dmy_hms()`**:          For          "day-month-year hour:minute:second".

**`mdy_hms()`**:          For          "month-day-year hour:minute:second".

```R
datetime_1 <- ymd_hms("2023-10-12 14:30:00") print(datetime_1) # [1] "2023-10-12 14:30:00 UTC"
```
```

3. Extracting Components

Once you have parsed dates and times, you may want to extract specific components such as year, month, day, or hour. The `lubridate` package provides functions for this purpose:

3.1 year(), month(), day(), hour(), minute(), second()

166

```R
# Extracting date-time components year_extracted <-
year(datetime_1) month_extracted <- month(datetime_1)
day_extracted <- day(datetime_1)

print(year_extracted)  # [1] 2023
print(month_extracted) # [1] 10
print(day_extracted)        # [1] 12
```

3.2 Weekday and Week

You can also obtain the corresponding weekday or week number:

```R
weekday_extracted <- wday(datetime_1) # 1: Sunday, 2:
Monday, ..., 7: Saturday week_number <-
week(datetime_1)

print(weekday_extracted) # [1] 5 (Friday)
print(week_number)       # [1] 41
```

4. Date-Time Arithmetic

Performing arithmetic operations with date-time objects is another key feature of `lubridate`. You can easily add or subtract time intervals.

```R
# Adding and subtracting time
```

167

```R
next_week <- datetime_1 + weeks(1) previous_hour <- datetime_1 - hours(1)

print(next_week)    # [1] "2023-10-19 14:30:00 UTC"

print(previous_hour)    # [1] "2023-10-12 13:30:00 UTC"
```

5. Time Zones

Handling time zones is critical in data analysis, especially if you are working with data collected from different regions. The `lubridate` package provides functions to deal with time zones effectively.

5.1 with_tz() and force_tz()

`with_tz()`: Converts the date-time object to a different time zone without changing the underlying moment.

`force_tz()`: Changes the time zone of a date-time object, altering the actual recorded time.

```R
# Time zone conversion

datetime_utc <- with_tz(datetime_1, "America/New_York") print(datetime_utc)    # Converts datetime to Eastern Time
```

6. Formatting Date-Time

After performing analyses, you may want to format date-time objects for presentation or output. The `lubridate` package allows you to format dates using `format()`.

```R
formatted_date <- format(datetime_1, "%B %d, %Y")
print(formatted_date)    # "October 12, 2023"
```

The `lubridate` package is an invaluable resource for R programmers dealing with date and time data. Its intuitive functions simplify parsing, extracting, manipulating, and formatting date-time objects, making it essential for effective data analysis.

Calculating Differences and Handling Time-Based Data

Understanding how to manipulate and calculate differences in time series data can reveal meaningful insights into trends, patterns, and behavioral changes over time.

In R programming, specialized packages and functions are available to facilitate the handling and analysis of time-based data. This chapter will explore these tools and techniques, providing a comprehensive guide on calculating differences in time-based data.

1. Understanding Time-Based Data in R

Time-based data, or time series data, consists of observations collected at successive points in time, often with a consistent frequency. Common examples include daily stock prices, monthly sales data, and annual temperature records.

In R, time-based data can be handled using several classes and packages, including:

Date: A basic R class for handling dates.

POSIXct and POSIXlt: Classes to manage date-time objects, allowing for both date and time manipulation.

lubridate: A powerful package designed to simplify dealing with dates and times in R.

zoo: A package that provides infrastructure for regular and irregular time series data. ### Example of Date and Date-Time Classes

```R
# Basic Date class

start_date <- as.Date("2023-01-01")  end_date <- as.Date("2023-12-31") print(start_date)

print(end_date)

# POSIXct for date-time

datetime_example <- as.POSIXct("2023-01-01 12:00:00") print(datetime_example)
```

2. Importing Time-Based Data

Often, time-based data is acquired through external sources such as CSV files or databases. R makes it easy to import these datasets and convert them into appropriate date-time formats.

Importing Data Example

```R
# Load necessary library library(readr)

# Import a CSV file with date data
data <- read_csv("time_series_data.csv")
# Convert a column to Date
data$date <- as.Date(data$date_column)
# Convert a column to POSIXct
data$datetime <- as.POSIXct(data$datetime_column)
```

3. Calculating Differences in Time-Based Data

Calculating differences between time points is crucial for understanding change over time. In R, you can easily compute differences using the `diff()` function and other related operations.

3.1 Simple Differences

The `diff()` function computes differences between consecutive observations in a numeric vector. When working with time data, be mindful that the output will be one less than the input.

```R
# Example time series data time_series <- c(100, 150, 200, 250)

# Calculate differences differences <- diff(time_series)
print(differences)
```

3.2 Differences in Time

Calculating differences in time can be performed using subtraction of date or date-time objects.

```R

# Example date vector

dates <- as.Date(c("2023-01-01", "2023-01-05", "2023-01-10"))

# Calculate the difference in days date_diff <- diff(dates)
print(date_diff)
```

3.3 Working with lubridate

The `lubridate` package offers functions for easier manipulation of date and time objects, enabling calculations like durations, intervals, and periods.

```R library(lubridate)

# Create example date-time objects start <- ymd("2023-01-01 08:00:00")

end <- ymd_hms("2023-01-01 10:30:00")


# Calculate duration

duration    <-    as.duration(difftime(end,    start))
print(duration)
```

4. Aggregating Time-Based Data

In many scenarios, it is essential to aggregate time series data to analyze trends efficiently. R provides tools like `aggregate()` and functions within the `dplyr` package to achieve this.

Example of Aggregating Monthly Data

```R
library(dplyr)

# Assume 'data' has columns 'date' and 'sales'
monthly_sales <- data %>%

group_by(month = floor_date(date, "month")) %>%
summarise(total_sales = sum(sales))
```

5. Visualization of Time-Based Data

Visual representation can aid in understanding trends and differences in time-based data. R offers various packages, such as `ggplot2`, for creating insightful visualizations.

Example of Time Series Plot

```R
library(ggplot2)

# Create a plot of monthly sales
ggplot(monthly_sales, aes(x = month, y = total_sales)) +
geom_line() +

labs(title = "Monthly Sales Over Time", x = "Month", y = "Total Sales")
```

Handling time-based data in R programming presents a wealth of opportunities for analysis and insight. By understanding date-time classes, calculating differences, aggregating data, and utilizing visualization techniques, analysts can unlock valuable information hidden within temporal data.

Conclusion

Congratulations! By reaching the end of "R Programming for Beginners: Master the Fundamentals of R, Even with Zero Coding Experience," you have embarked on an exciting journey into the world of data analysis and programming. You've taken the first steps towards mastering R, a powerful and versatile language used by data scientists, statisticians, and analysts worldwide.

Throughout this book, we have covered the essential concepts of R programming, from installation and basic syntax to working with data frames and visualizing data. By now, you should feel comfortable writing and executing R scripts, performing data manipulation, and creating visual representations of your findings. You've learned how to tackle real-world problems using data, a skill that is increasingly valuable in today's data-driven environment.

Remember that learning R, like any skill, takes time and practice. Don't be discouraged if you encounter challenges along the way; they are part of the learning process. The key is to stay curious and keep experimenting with new datasets and projects. Consider joining online communities, forums, or local meetups where you can share your experiences, ask questions, and learn from others. Collaboration and discussion with fellow learners can enhance your understanding and spark new ideas.

As you continue your journey, explore additional resources—books, online courses, and tutorials—that can deepen your knowledge and broaden your expertise. R has a rich ecosystem of packages and libraries that extend its capabilities, making it a robust tool for statistical analysis, machine learning, and data visualization. The more you practice and engage with the R community, the more confident you will become.

In summary, you now possess the foundational skills to navigate the world of R programming and apply your knowledge to real-world situations. Whether you aspire to be a data analyst, researcher, or simply want to enhance your data skills, the possibilities are endless. Embrace the challenges, celebrate your achievements, and never stop learning.

Thank you for choosing this book as your guide. We wish you all the best in your R programming journey. Happy coding!

Biography

Peter Simon is a passionate explorer of patterns, possibilities, and the profound power of data. With a deep-rooted love for *Simon*—the very subject of this eBook—Peter brings a unique blend of technical expertise and creative insight to his writing. His journey began in the world of numbers and logic, where he discovered that behind every dataset lies a story waiting to be told.

Armed with a background in data science and a mastery of tools like R programming and machine learning, Peter has spent years diving into the intricacies of data analysis to uncover meaning, drive innovation, and solve real-world problems. Whether he's building predictive models or visualizing complex insights, his work is guided by curiosity and a desire to make knowledge accessible and impactful.

When he's not immersed in code or statistical models, Peter enjoys exploring the crossroads of technology and creativity. He finds inspiration in teaching others, mentoring aspiring data scientists, and contributing to open-source projects that push the boundaries of what's possible.

This eBook is a reflection of Peter's passion—for Simon, for science, and for the transformative power of understanding. His goal is simple: to empower you with the tools and insights to explore new horizons, just as he has.

Glossary: R Programming for Beginners

A

Algorithm

A step-by-step procedure or formula for solving a problem. In R, algorithms are often implemented in the form of functions for data analysis, statistical modeling, or machine learning.

API (Application Programming Interface)

A set of rules and protocols that allows different software applications to communicate with each other. R can interact with various APIs to retrieve or send data.

B

Base R

Refers to the default functions and datasets that come with R when it is installed. Base R provides fundamental capabilities without the need for additional packages.

Bibliography

A list of references or sources used in research or analysis. In many R projects, a bibliography may be included to cite data sources or related studies.

C

Code

The written instructions that are executed by the R interpreter. Code is typically written in R scripts or RMarkdown files.

Data Frame

A two-dimensional, table-like structure in R used for storing data. A data frame can hold different types of variables (numeric, character, etc.), similar to a spreadsheet.

Function

A block of code designed to perform a specific task. Functions in R can be built-in, like `mean()` and

`sum()`, or user-defined, allowing for modular programming. ## D

Debugging

The process of identifying and fixing errors in your R code. Debugging is essential for ensuring that your code runs as intended.

DPLYR

An R package that provides a grammar for data manipulation, allowing users to easily filter, select, summarize, and arrange data.

E

Environment

In R, an environment refers to a collection of objects (variables, functions) created during a session. The Global Environment is where user-defined objects reside.

Exporting

The process of saving data or R objects to an external file format (e.g., CSV, Excel) for use outside R. ## F

Package

A collection of R functions, data, and documentation bundled together to provide specific functionality. CRAN (Comprehensive R Archive Network) hosts thousands of R packages.

Plotting

The creation of visual representations (like graphs and charts) of data. R has robust plotting capabilities through base graphics and additional packages like `ggplot2`.

G

GGPlot2

An R package for data visualization that implements the Grammar of Graphics, allowing users to create complex, multi-layered visualizations with ease.

H

Histogram

A graphical representation of the distribution of a dataset. Histograms divide the data into bins and display the frequency of observations in each bin.

I

Iteration

The process of looping through a set of values or objects, commonly achieved with `for`, `while`, or `apply` functions in R.

Importing

The act of bringing external data into R from various file types (such as CSV, RData, or Excel) for analysis. ## J

JSON (JavaScript Object Notation)

A lightweight data interchange format that is easy for humans to read and write and easy for machines to parse and generate. R can read and write JSON using packages like `jsonlite`.

K

Kernel

In the context of R, a kernel often refers to the R interpreter running in an environment like RStudio, which processes R code.

L

Libraries

A folder or collection of packages in R. When you install a package, it is usually stored in a library that R accesses for functions and data.

179

M

Matrix

A two-dimensional, homogeneous data structure in R made up of elements of the same type, used extensively in mathematical and statistical computations.

Modeling

The process of creating a statistical model to describe or predict outcomes based on data. R provides many functions for modeling, including linear regression.

N

NA (Not Available)

A placeholder for missing values in R. R handles NA differently from other values, so explicit care is needed when analyzing data containing NAs.

O

Object

A fundamental building block in R, which can be a variable, function, or data structure. Everything in R (including functions) is treated as an object.

P

Plot

A graphical representation of data, which can include scatterplots, line graphs, bar charts, and more. Plots are essential for data analysis and visualization.

Q

Quantile

A statistical measure that divides a dataset into equal segments. In R, the `quantile()` function can be used to calculate quantiles for a given numeric vector.

R

RStudio

An integrated development environment (IDE) specifically for R that provides tools for writing code, visualizing data, and managing projects more efficiently.

Repository

A storage location for datasets, packages, or code. CRAN is a repository for R packages, while GitHub serves as a repository for code sharing and collaboration.

S

Script

A text file containing a series of R commands. Scripts allow for automation of code execution, making it easier to reproduce analyses.

Statistical Analysis

The application of statistical methods to understand data, including descriptive statistics, inferential statistics, and hypothesis testing.

T

Tidyverse

A collection of R packages designed for data science that

share a common philosophy and grammar. Key packages include `ggplot2`, `dplyr`, `tidyr`, and more.

Vector

A one-dimensional array that can hold multiple values of the same type in R. Vectors are essential for data manipulation and analysis.

U

User-Defined Function

A custom function created by the user in R to perform specific tasks, enhancing reusability and organization in code.

V

Variable

A named storage location in R that holds data. Variables can store different data types, including numeric, character, and logical.

W

Workspace

The collection of all objects in R's memory during a session. The workspace can be saved and restored, preserving your work for future sessions.

WRDS (Wharton Research Data Services)

A comprehensive data management service providing access to a variety of business, financial, and economic data, often used in academic research and teaching.

X

XML (eXtensible Markup Language)

A markup language that defines rules for encoding documents. R can read and write XML files using the

`xml2` package, enabling data interchange with web services. ## Y

Y-Variable

In statistical modeling, the dependent variable whose value is predicted based on other variables (independent variables). It is often plotted on the vertical axis.

www.ingramcontent.com/pod-product-compliance
Lightning Source LLC
LaVergne TN
LVHW051335050326
832903LV00031B/3553

* 9 7 9 8 3 1 9 1 0 5 2 4 0 *